Writer, meditation teacher and mama of three Caitlin Cady is the author of *Heavily Meditated: Your Down-to-Earth Guide to Learning Meditation and Getting High on Life* and the creator of the Heavily Meditated app. Caitlin has been called a 'wellbeing whiz' by *Australian Yoga Journal*, and her work has been featured in *Women's Health*, *Marie Claire*, *Real Living*, *Vogue*, *Prevention* and *Body + Soul*. Caitlin's positive perspectives and relatable, playful approach have inspired people across the globe to get lit up and start living to their full potential. Connect with Caitlin on Instagram @caitlincady or her site caitlincady.com.

THE HOPE DEALER

CAITLIN CADY

HAY HOUSE

Carlsbad, California • New York City
London • Sydney • New Delhi

First published and distributed in Australia by:
Affirm Press, Boon Wurrung Country, 28 Thistlewaite Street,
South Melbourne, VIC 3205
Tel: (03) 8695 9623; www.affirmpress.com.au

Published in the United Kingdom by:
Hay House UK Ltd, The Sixth Floor, Watson House,
54 Baker Street, London W1U 7BU
Tel: +44 (0)20 3927 7290; Fax: +44 (0)20 3927 7291; www.hayhouse.co.uk

Published in the United States of America by:
Hay House Inc., PO Box 5100, Carlsbad, CA 92018-5100
Tel: (1) 760 431 7695 or (800) 654 5126
Fax: (1) 760 431 6948 or (800) 650 5115; www.hayhouse.com

Cover and interior design: Dani Hunt, Neverland Studio
Typeset in FreightText Pro 10/15

A catalogue record for this book is available from the British Library.

Tradepaper ISBN: 978-1-83782-187-7
E-book ISBN: 978-1-4019-7654-5

Printed and bound by CPI Group (UK) Ltd, Croydon, CR0 4YY

MIX
Paper | Supporting
responsible forestry
FSC
www.fsc.org   FSC® C171272

☾

For my mama, who makes life magic.
For my papa, who taught me how to wonder.

I acknowledge the people of the Bundjalung Nation, the traditional custodians of the land where this book was written. I honour all Aboriginal and Torres Strait Islander peoples and recognise their rich tradition of storytelling and wisdom, and their continuing connection to land, waters and culture. I pay my deepest respects to Elders past, present and emerging.

I believe inspiration has the power to change us. It can spark our imagination, stir the creative forces within us and spur us into action, thereby altering the course of our lives. Inspiration is what motivates us to create – be it art, food, music, poetry or change within ourselves or the world around us. Inspiration sustains us, excites us and empowers us to think, feel and act in new ways. It helps us to see things differently, to open our imagination to new possibilities.

When we open ourselves to new possibilities, we reconnect with a sense of hope. Hope is, after all, a form of inspiration – and a potent one at that. Hope has the dual role of not only inspiring us, but also inviting us to *trust*. Our highest hopes are always rooted in a longing for positive change *and* the belief that change is possible. In fact, the word 'hope' itself is imbued with a sense of trust and confidence: one of its origins is the Old English word *hopa*, meaning 'confidence in the future'.

It is my own hope that this book inspires you and gives you confidence in the future. The pages that follow are full of perspectives, prompts and questions that invite you to relate to things like rejection, sorrow, stuckness, self-doubt, emptiness, vulnerability and grief in new, empowering and *hopeful* ways.

My intention is that these words inspire you to set fire to limiting beliefs, reframe resistance and rejection, and say sayonara to self-doubt and perfectionism while building intuition, resilience, courage and compassion. The messages are intended to help you reconnect with a sense of positivity and self-trust, so that you can tune in to your highest, most hopeful self. Every. Single. Day. No matter what comes your way.

A RITUAL FOR DAILY INSPIRATION

On that note, I invite you to use this book as a tool for daily ritual.

Ritual lifts the veil on the divine – the universe, nature, Goddess, God or however you like to describe it. It reminds us how sacred and precious this life is. It gifts us the opportunity to weave the themes, symbols and learnings of our journey into a rich tapestry of understanding and resonance that we can wrap ourselves in. It crowns us with connection and elevated thinking so that we can continue to tune in to our higher knowing and intuition – the voice of our highest self.

When we are led by the compass of inner guidance we can move forwards with sure-footedness, knowing that we are heard, seen and supported by something greater than ourselves.

It's so easy to stay on the surface and skip over the deep currents of life. But my invitation to you is to carve out a sacred space in your day for a ritual that includes stillness and silence, as well as reflection and inspiration. A simple daily ritual that includes these elements can help forge a path towards a life infused with ever-deepening understanding, meaning and joy: a life filled with hope, courage and limitless possibilities.

Here are three ways you might like to weave this book into a regular ritual for a daily dose of guidance and inspiration. After meditation is an ideal time to pick up this book, no matter which method you choose!

1. GET A HIT OF INSPIRATION FOR YOUR DAY

In preparation for the day ahead, take a few moments to become quiet and turn your gaze inward. You might mentally say to yourself, 'Please show me a message that will serve me well today.' With that intention in your heart, let your fingertips intuitively lead you to the perfect page for your day.

2. SEEK GUIDANCE

You can also use this book to get a little guidance on a particular question or situation that is present for you. It's best to focus on one matter at a time. Take a few moments to quieten your mind and turn your gaze inward. Then, keeping your eyes closed, reflect on the question or situation you'd like to shed light on. You might mentally say to yourself, 'Please show me a perspective that would serve me in this situation.' With the question held in your heart, run your fingers along the pages of the book until you feel called to pause, fan the book open and place your finger on a page or simply let the book fall open to a page.

3. TAKE IT AS IT COMES

Another approach is to read the messages in the sequence they are presented in the book, taking in one message each day for 101 days. This is an effortless and elegant way to receive inspiration day by day.

Sit with it

Once you've read your message for the day, take some time to sit with it. You might like to spend a few minutes journalling or take a photo of the words and revisit them later. You might also like to leave the book open to the message you received so that you can check in with it throughout the day. (Propping it up on an easel at your desk or on your dresser is a beautiful way to do this!)

No matter which way you pick a page, know that there is no wrong way. Simply trust in yourself and be open to a sense of divine timing. Resonant symbols, serendipitous signs and meaningful messages present themselves when we simply pay attention.

With big love, good vibes and highest hopes from my heart to yours,

Caitlin x

inspir

aw

ation
nits

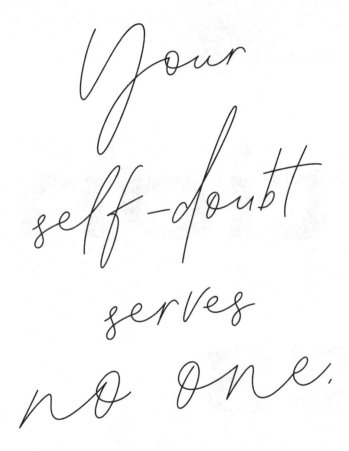

Your self-doubt serves no one.

Sharing your gifts can
serve many.

YOUR SELF-DOUBT SERVES NO ONE.
SHARING YOUR GIFTS CAN SERVE MANY.

I t's not your job to judge what you have to share. It's not your job to struggle against your gifts or try to sort and label them accurately. It's not your job to silently whisper the word 'imposter' enough times that you start to believe it. It's not your job to withhold or second-guess or doubt whether what you have is good enough.

None of that is your job. None of it is even any of your *business*. Your job is to share what you have to share, to be a good steward of your gifts.

So stop judging your gifts and start sharing them.

If you believe that your gifts are actually gifts – streams from the infinite, treasures loaned to you for this lifetime by the divine – then who are you *not* to share what you have?

Stop asking 'Who am I to ...?' 'Who am I to call myself an artist? Who am I to call myself a teacher? Who am I to publish this poem? Who am I to put a price like this on my work? Who am I to use my voice? Who am I to be seen? Who am I to love myself? Who am I to dream a dream that big? Who am I to feel worthy and good enough?'

Instead, ask yourself, 'Who am I *not* to ...?'

Sharing your gifts with the world is being in service to the divine. You are a vessel, a channel, a note in the symphony of the universe expressing itself. When you stifle that natural flow (yes, it is natural!) with the question 'Who am I to ...?' you stomp on the seeds of providence.

Stop stomping. Stop sitting on your inheritance of inborn divinity. Stop stagnating the flow of miraculousness within you. Stop doubting your worthiness.

Your self-doubt serves no one. Sharing your gifts can serve many.

So get out there! Be bold. Be brave. Be audacious. Be of service. Be generous. Share your little dash of infinity. Offer up your gifts, because they are divine. Stop asking 'Who am I to ...?' and start asking 'Who am I *not* to ...?'

We are waiting for your magic.

RESISTANCE IS A
GREAT SIGN, NOT A
STOP SIGN

I f there is something you are resisting right now, take note: whatever you are resisting is probably a pathway to your full potential. The greater the resistance, the greater the opportunity. The role of resistance is to keep you in the known, where you feel safe and comfortable. Nonetheless, resistance is an important messenger. You just need to learn to interpret the signals correctly.

When you notice resistance pop up (it looks like procrastination, self-doubt, self-sabotage, seeking out distractions, waffling and hesitation), pay attention. Look it in the eye. But instead of interpreting it as a bad sign ('This isn't the right thing for me' or 'Maybe the timing just isn't right' or 'I guess I'm not really cut out for this' or 'See, I'm not good enough or worthy enough'), start to see it as a *great* sign. Resistance isn't a sign that you should stop. It's a sign that you should *go*. It's a signal that you're really onto something.

Resistance tells you that whatever stands before you is a bona fide opportunity. A call for expansion. A shot at showing up and shining in a wonderful new way. Resistance is a beacon, guiding you towards actualising everything you are capable of: your full potential.

So when you next notice resistance pop up, don't back down. Give yourself the go-ahead. Stop wasting all that energy dancing around the fire of resistance and instead, walk through it. Let the flames burn away your doubt and fear. What will be left is the truth of you: limitless possibility, boundless will, courageous action.

Once you break through the seal of resistance, the rest is easy. You'll be unstoppable. And when resistance shows up again, you'll know what to do: *break through*. Moving through resistance is like exercising a muscle. Every time you choose to walk through resistance, you melt another layer of self-doubt and build your strength and resolve. You up-level. You progress. You get closer to your highest self.

So, my friend, it's time to stop letting resistance run your shit. Bite the bullet. Sketch it out. Make the call. Write the words. Press 'send'. Raise your hand. Start the damn thing. Finish the damn thing.

Because you are bigger than the resistance you feel. And your full potential is waiting on the other side.

SEEING THE BEST IN *others* HELPS THEM SEE THE BEST IN *themselves*

SEEING THE BEST IN OTHERS HELPS THEM SEE THE BEST IN THEMSELVES.

When we are reminded of our goodness, our magic and the ways we matter, it helps us to be our best selves. And when we all show up as our best selves, the world changes for the better.

Yet we seem collectively obsessed with criticism and catching one another being 'bad'. We seem totally fixated on finding wrongness in others as if, by default, others being 'wrong' makes us 'right'.

What if we redirected our focus? What if we rebelled against this current of criticism and judgement? How might we change the world for the better, by simply reminding each other of our goodness?

Here's my invitation to us all:

See the good. When you see it, speak it.

More blessing. Less bashing.

More congratulations. Less criticism.

More big ups. Less putting-down.

Choose to be a loving mirror. Reflect someone's light back to them.

Seeing the best in people helps them see the best in themselves. So go out there and see who you can catch being good today.

THANK

SORROW

FOR

HER GIFTS

I f there is something you are mourning, if there is grief or sadness that has cut you open, remember that when sorrow comes to visit, she brings precious gifts with her. Gifts of healing. Gifts of perspective.

Sorrow is an alchemist, making medicine out of our pain. She sutures and spreads balm on old wounds, mending relationships that are frayed, broken, busted and weary.

Sorrow casts a sweet spell of humility. She lets the words 'I'm sorry' or 'I forgive you' burst into bloom in our hearts and spill out of our mouths.

Sorrow inspires us to leap over the gaps in our lives where bridges have been burned. Sorrow awakens us to our wings, reminds us that we can always soar away from contempt, anger and blame, over the river of judgement, and land softly on the banks of understanding.

Sorrow reminds us that in the equation of a life, the bottom line is love. Not things. Not awards. Not money. Not our dress size. Not how much we have achieved. Not who was right or who was wrong.

The bottom line is how well you listened. How freely you gave. How joyfully you served. How generous you were. How patient. How grateful. How you made people feel. How much room you made in your heart. How many tender moments you had.

Of course, next to these gifts of healing and perspective, sorrow also holds within her the sharp spurs of regret. These barbed messengers teach us that we can do better. So do better while you have the time, before your life slips through your fingers.

Thank sorrow for her gifts. Let her remind you of how precious this life is. How fleeting. How changeable. Honour her by accepting these gifts. Let them illuminate and soften any grievances calcifying the tightly wound helix of your heart.

Start right now. Gather this moment up in your arms. Wrap it in the embrace of your full attention. Listen well. Love well. Be exquisitely tender, patient and grateful. Make time. Become a bridge. Lay down the heavy armour of judgement. Say 'I'm sorry' like it's a prayer.

Remember that we only ever have two options: love or fear. Remember that this life is only ever for loving. Remember that loving and giving are the only ways to make a life matter.

BUSYNESS IS NOT

A BADGE OF HONOUR

BUSYNESS IS NOT A BADGE OF HONOUR.

B usyness is not synonymous with worthiness. Busyness is not a status symbol. So let's stop treating it as such.

Let's stop making 'busy' our default response to the question 'How have you been?' 'Busy' is not only a lazy (and boring) way of summing up our lives, but it creates an internal climate of overwhelm and perpetuates the cultural conditioning of fatigue and burnout.

You don't need an excuse, a reason or permission to rest. You don't owe us an explanation. You don't need to wait until you get sick to stop. You don't need to wait until you're burned out to take a break.

Reclaim agency over your energy. Ride your cycles of vitality like the waves they are. Rebel against the artificial currents of urgency and importance.

Rest is an inherent part of the natural world. All around us things ebb, flow, rise, fall, frost, melt, shine and hibernate. As human beings, why would we be excluded from this law of nature?

Rest is rich with merit; and yet, our contemporary culture has discouraged us from having it, instructing us to override our instincts and push forwards in a perpetual hustle. We've gone so far as to turn busyness into a badge of honour and to twist rest into a source of shame.

But that's a losing proposition. We're overriding our natural rhythms instead of embracing their wisdom. When we should be rising and falling like the seasons, the moon and the tides, we're burning ourselves out, buzzing and flickering erratically like cheap neon lights.

We've forgotten how to rest. In fact, many of us are downright scared of rest. And yet, without rest, we can't really do, be or achieve our best.

So let's reclaim rest, shall we? Because we all do our best when we let ourselves rest.

REJECTION *is a* REDIRECTION

REJECTION IS A REDIRECTION.

No. It's a word many of us live in fear of. We habitually misinterpret rejection as a bad thing – a source of shame; proof of our unsatisfactory skills, services or self.

But what if we stopped seeing rejection as evidence of our inadequacy? What if we stopped seeing rejection as a lost opportunity?

What if rejection is just a redirection? What if the brush-off, the rebuff, the thumbs down and the cold shoulder are all just signposts pointing you back to the path that's right for you?

What if rejection is a redirection away from what won't work towards what will? What if rejection is not a lost opportunity but rather a favourable circumstance – a chance to conserve energy and resources for something more aligned, more fertile, more fruitful?

Flipping the script on rejection makes hearing 'no' more of a relief and less of a letdown. With practice, we become more neutral in response to 'no'. And when we're more neutral to 'no', we can be more resilient and braver with our lives.

Because (listen up!) rejection is a byproduct of bravery. Rejection only happens when you're putting yourself out there. Rejection only happens when you're putting your hand up or making an offer or throwing out an idea or asking a question.

Rejection doesn't happen to people who are hiding and doubting and shrinking. Those people are living in fear of rejection, which stunts their curiosity, their creativity, their courage and their conviction. In my book, that's a downright dastardly way to waste our days here on earth.

So stop taking rejection personally. Remember that if you're being rejected, it means you're living a brave life. Start seeing rejection as a redirection.

YIELDING YIELDS GREAT RETURNS

YIELDING YIELDS GREAT RETURNS.

A change of plans, a shift in energy, an alteration to our timelines, a shuffling of priorities. These things happen every day in ways big and small. And every time, we must make a choice. We can choose to collapse under the weight of the change; we can fight it. Or we can *meet it*. This middle path, meeting what is, could also be called yielding, and it's the path of catharsis, growth and expansion. In other words, it's the way forwards.

Yielding is not giving up and lying down. It's bending, not breaking. It is a willingness to meet yourself where you are, gracefully giving way to what *is*. Yielding is what allows you to make space for expansion in your life, heart and body.

The fact is that yielding yields great returns. It fosters fresh perspectives and gifts us with dynamic healing, robust intuition and inspiration. It invites the growth of something new, something tender, something unexpected.

Meet yourself where you are (right now) and you'll understand trust – in yourself and in life.

Meet your body where it is (and exactly as it is) and you'll discover oceans of gratitude for the miracle that you are. Meet others where they are and you'll come face to face with the blossoming of mutual compassion, forgiveness and resonance.

This is grace. This is trust. This is yielding.

WHAT ARE YOU

WITHHOLDING BECAUSE

YOU'RE AFRAID IT'S NOT

GOOD ENOUGH?

WHAT ARE YOU WITHHOLDING BECAUSE YOU'RE AFRAID IT'S NOT GOOD ENOUGH?

What are you refusing to give? What project are you stalling on? What are you unwilling to take action on? What are you holding back until it's more done? More finished? More certain? More loveable? More figured out? More timely? More professional? More beautiful? More perfect?

Here's the thing: at a certain point, withholding your gifts, your love, your joy, your voice, your opinion, your knowledge, your intuition, your art, your work, your affection, your vulnerability, your realness, your perspective and your truth becomes selfish.

Who are you to say what's good enough? You're not an expert in what other people need or want. So what the f*ck are you so afraid of? Anticipating that it's not going to land well? Or that it could be better?

No amount of revision can protect you from the risk that your gifts won't be received well by everyone. But that's okay! You are not for everyone, but you are for a lot of people. So don't hold out on them.

These people need what you have. And by waiting for whatever you have to be refined down to some pristine, polished piece of perfection (which, newsflash, doesn't actually exist), you're letting your ego and your fear of 'not enough' stifle the gift of sharing.

When you deem yourself the judge of what's good enough to print, publish or push play on, it's more than likely that the manuscript will gather dust on your desk, the canvas will go unpainted, the idea will be voiceless and the person will never know how they lit you up. That's a lot of unfulfilled potential left on the table. For you. For everyone.

There are run-on effects from your failure to launch. Who will never know how deeply they mattered? Who will never be inspired by your voice or your action? Who misses out? *We all do.*

So stop secreting it away. Stop hiding. Stop stagnating. Stop stifling. Stop sitting on it. Stop containing. Remember that done is better than perfect. Remember that perfect never comes.

Go on now. Get busy. You've got things to share, say and make. And we're waiting for you.

LET IT BE AN

EXPERIMENT

EXPERIMENT

LET IT BE AN

EXPERIMENT

EXPERIMENT

LET IT BE AN EXPERIMENT.

H ere's a recipe for a predictable life: play it safe. Stick to the rules. Hang close to what's been tried and tested. Insist on particular outcomes. Deem all other conclusions a failure. Also: prepare yourself for boredom (because predictability is safe but tedious) and disappointment (because you can rarely control the outcome anyway).

Or: let it be an experiment. All of it: the relationship, the painting, the poem, the partnership, the business idea, the meditation.

To experiment is to be captivated by the joy and playfulness of possibility. To have the courage to tune in to your instincts, sift through the possibilities and commit to just one (for now). To detach yourself from outcomes and free yourself from the confinement of expectation, bias or judgement. To have the willingness to watch what unfolds with wonder and amazement. To open yourself to seeing the unseen. To welcome revelation.

The best experiments aren't engineered to produce a specific outcome. They are bold leaps, fortified with intention and derived from curiosity – not expectation. The best experiments test ideas and trust that the truth remains to be seen. They are a process of discovery, not a mission with a map and marching orders.

Experimentation is an opportunity, not an obligation. If the experiment fails, you're not a failure, because the purpose wasn't to produce a particular outcome – it was to discover something new. Experimentation is an audacious adventure into the unknown, designed by a curious mind, executed with a courageous heart and fuelled by a daring spirit.

My advice? Throw out the rules. Trade in the polished outcomes. Blow off the hedged bets and calculated expectations. Choose mystery. Head towards uncharted waters. Feel the electrical charge created by fear and possibility – that marriage of opposites that makes up the unknown. Embrace that eager giddiness of discovery. Brew up big ideas. Mine your instincts. Arm yourself with wonder. Give it a go.

Let your life be a love affair with curiosity and courage. Let it be a wonderful experiment.

ASKING
FOR
HELP IS
A FORM
OF
PRAYER

ASKING FOR HELP IS A FORM OF PRAYER.

Asking for help is not a display of weakness or proof that you've failed. Asking for help is a courageous confession of the facts as they are. It's a commitment to the truth and the courage to tell it as it is. It's giving voice to a desire, hope or wish. It's a display of trust. It's humility over ego. It's communion with your community.

Above all, asking for help is a form of prayer. Because prayer is all of these things: confession, petition, hope, trust, communion. Prayer is sometimes *please* and sometimes *thank you*, and usually both. Prayer is an appeal for love.

By asking for help, you are issuing a divine invitation: giving someone else the opportunity to serve and share their gifts. This exchange of giving and receiving helps bring you and the other person closer together. Telling the truth – that we need each other and that we are in this together – is raw, irresistible and magnetic. Sharing the gifts of our strengths lightens the burdens of our weaknesses. Giving and receiving help in any form is a redirection of the abundance of unique resources bestowed on each of us. What is more beautiful, more divine, than that?

So let's stop shaming ourselves out of telling the truth. Let's stop the self-judgement and shut down the belief that we have to do it all on our own.

You can't do everything. You aren't good at everything. You're meant to ask for help, and you're meant to pitch in and share your gifts. Both are noble. Both are necessary. Both are in service of the divine.

LET YOUR HEART

LEAD THE WAY

LET YOUR HEART LEAD THE WAY.

If we want our lives to change, we need to be willing to make different decisions. But to make different decisions, we have to shake up *how* we make them.

What if you burned down the clever plans your mind has concocted?

What if you shredded the spreadsheets with their tight calculations of output and input?

What if you dropped the metrics and the carefully measured columns of pros and cons?

What if you hit mute on outside advice?

What if you laid aside the lens of fear?

What if you put down what feels heavy?

What if, instead, you let your heart lead a revolution in your life?

What if you made your decisions by how they feel, not how they look?

What if you calculated what you can give, rather than what you can get?

What if you gazed through the lens of love?

What if you gave heed to your gut instinct?

What if you picked up the choice that felt lightest?

What if you followed joy?

What if you let your heart lead the way?

Try it for a day, a week, a month or the rest of your life. Guaranteed: make your decisions differently and you will make different decisions. Likely: integrity will be effortless, boundaries will be honoured, joy will be created. That means less stress, more happiness and more alignment.

Go on now. Shake it up. Let your heart take the lead.

Shift the feeling *first*

D id you know that simply by smiling you trigger a chemical reaction in your brain that boosts your mood, lowers stress and relieves pain? It's true, and there is plenty of scientific research to prove it. It's a pretty radical cycle: smile more and you'll feel more like smiling.

What if you apply that formula to your feelings, too? Just as your smile can send a signal to your brain, your feelings can send a signal to your future.

Old, familiar feelings of the unhelpful variety keep you linked to the past. And when you're stuck repeating and recycling old feelings, your future will reflect your past.

On the other hand, you can consciously create forward momentum and forecast future feels by shifting your feelings. In short: feel good more and you'll have more to feel good about.

Here's a simple way to start. Next time you're feeling negative or stuck in the mud, swap out the feeling for something better. Just like that feature in your Word document: find and replace.

Here's a list of simple swaps you can make that will upgrade your current (and future) feels:

DELETE THIS	FOR THIS	DELETE THIS	FOR THIS
fear	trust	exhaustion	energy
overwhelm	spaciousness	stuckness	flow
loneliness	connection	anxiety	calm
no time	plenty of time	worry	freedom
sadness	gratitude	scarcity	abundance

Every time you feel the old, unhelpful, undesired feeling, consciously delete and replace it. Just noticing the negative feeling and mentally repeating its positive opposite is enough to make you feel a difference.

Shift the feeling first. The rest will follow. And smile while you're at it, will ya?

MAKE PLEASURE

A PRIORITY

MAKE PLEASURE A PRIORITY.

When my great-grandmother Josephine gave her granddaughters money for their birthdays, she'd hand over the crisp bills with an appeal: 'Don't spend it on groceries.'

She didn't tell her granddaughters to save the money for a rainy day or to spend it wisely. Instead, she told them not to fritter away the gift on day-to-day essentials like bread or toilet paper. She not only gave the girls permission to spend the money on something fun, something beautiful, something pleasurable, something unnecessary – she actually *required* them to.

You can apply this same advice to the gift of time and how you spend it. When you find yourself with an hour of free time, in a quiet house without appointments, plans or urgent to-dos, how do you spend it? Doing something practical and necessary? Clearing your inbox? Folding laundry? Catching up on text messages? Cleaning out the fridge? Re-organising your kid's sock drawer?

If so, here's my invitation to you: when you next find yourself with the gift of time, *don't spend it on groceries.*

Instead, treat yo self. Do something indulgent, something beautiful. Something that has nothing to do with practicality or necessity. Take a bath in the afternoon. Page through a book of poetry. Get out that old palette of paints. Do a puzzle. Make a cup of tea and call your best friend. Get back in bed and eat a chocolate croissant. Watch reruns of *Sex and the City* in your undies. Play. Relax. Enjoy. Truly treat yourself.

What's amazing about this approach is that when you free yourself from practical concerns and responsibilities and, instead, make pleasure the priority, it renews you. It liberates you from the grind of the mundane and lifts you up. It's an investment in joy. And that, my friend, pays dividends that productivity (tidy sock drawer, I'm looking at you!) never will.

BELONG TO THOSE WHO BLESS YOU WITH THEIR BELIEF IN YOU

BELONG TO THOSE WHO BLESS YOU WITH THEIR
BELIEF IN YOU.

S urround yourself with people who love you as you are, right now,
but will also dream with you about what's next. The ones who let
you be as you are *and* let you grow into the full expansion of yourself.

Surround yourself with people who know you are already enough,
and also that you're just getting started.

Surround yourself with people who see your potential and sing your
magic back to you when you forget the tune.

Surround yourself with people who take you by the hands, look you
in the eyes and say, 'I believe in you. I believe in your ideas. I know just
how much you have to give.'

Say so long to the people who keep you small. Surround yourself
with people who help you expand.

Belong to those who bless you with their belief in you.

Don't let self-doubt drown your dreams.

Don't let self-doubt drown your dreams.

Don't let self-doubt drown your dreams.

Don't let self-doubt drown your dreams.

Y ou've probably heard this question before: 'What would you do if you could not fail?' It has its merits as a prompt. It's a big-picture question, which is helpful for generating big-picture answers. It reminds us just how large a role failure plays in our dreams. It pulls back the curtain on our deeply held fear of failure and offers a glimpse into the world beyond it – a world where we have the courage to live to our full potential.

But the question is also a little saccharine, because it skates over the surface of the underlying issue: how to navigate the fear of failure itself. Plus, it's unrealistic. The critical thinkers and sceptics among us hear that question and, with a roll of the eyes, think, '*Cute* question'. And they're right.

Because guess what? Failure is actually inevitable. We're all going to fail some of the time. And, truthfully, failure gets a bad rap. We'd never evolve, learn or hone our craft if it weren't for the failures in our lives.

For the record, failure is not usually that bad, friend. The fear of failure is often worse than the actual failure. So instead of using *not failing* as a framework for dreaming, maybe we just need to adjust our tolerance for failure and turn down the volume on our fear of it.

What does the fear of failure sound like? It sounds like self-doubt. Self-doubt is the voice of fear that says we shouldn't or can't do the things that move us towards our full potential. It's the culprit that keeps us small, stuck and quiet.

Think about how much energy you waste in dialogue with self-doubt. For most of us, it's a phenomenal amount. And now imagine if you redirected that energy into dialoguing with your dreams – or, better yet, just doing the things (instead of worrying about whether you *should* and what might happen if you *do*).

The truth is, you already have the courage and conviction you need to live your dreams and expand to your full potential. It's there, within you, all the time – but your persistent negative self-talk and second-guessing just drown it out.

So where to from here? Hit mute on self-doubt for a day. When self-doubt's trash talk pops up, 'X' it out. Dial that shit down.   >

Hit unsubscribe. Unfollow. Delete, delete, delete. Then replace the thought with something useful and positive. (If you're not sure what to replace it with, a reliable option is usually the *opposite* of whatever the self-doubt is saying.)

Then, take note of what happens – how you move through the world. What steps you take. What decisions you own. Where you go. How much more energy you have to devote to your dreams. How you feel. How you engage with others. What you require from them. (Hint: it will be less. When you're not drowning in self-doubt, you need a whole lot less outside validation.) Notice who you are, *sans* the self-doubt.

If you notice a difference (and you will), choose to make it a habit. In time, self-belief and positivity will be your new defaults. And self-doubt will be out of a job – the poor sucker.

So start now. Try it. You're the DJ. Choose to hit mute on self-doubt. Select a different track. Tune in to the potential within you and let it sing out. It's the song of your becoming, and it's really f*cking beautiful.

MAKE WAVES OF LOVE

MAKE WAVES OF LOVE

MAKE WAVES OF LOVE

MAKE WAVES OF LOVE.

D id you wake up uninspired, unmotivated or in a downright funk? Shake it off with one question: 'How can I be of service today?'

When we shift our focus to how we can serve, we disconnect from our ego and reconnect to our divinity. We break free of the confines of our brain and take a swan dive into our heart. We swap contraction in favour of expansion. We let go of the idea that our happiness is conditional on getting, having or achieving. We shift away from the question 'What can I get?' and towards 'What can I give?'

This isn't about overachieving, giving in the hope of getting, or people pleasing. It's about remembering that we are all here for a reason (to serve) and that we all have the capability and responsibility to live that destiny. You were given the *gift* of this life for a reason. You are a creation of the divine. You matter. And you can make a difference in someone's day today.

When you make waves of love, service and generosity in this ocean of consciousness we all share, you lift others up and guide them towards making their own positive contributions.

So do it. Unstick yourself. Prise yourself loose from the grip of melancholy and malaise and, instead, rise up and remember the ripple effect you create in the world. Ask how you can serve. Then make some beautiful waves today.

Let's be our best for each other.

Even on the good days.

LET'S BE OUR BEST FOR EACH OTHER.
EVEN ON THE GOOD DAYS.

It's beautiful how we really show up for each other when things are tough – those unimaginably hard times. Like when unwanted news lands at our feet, when hard choices have to be made, when illness brings us to our knees or when life is lost and someone we love is stolen away too soon.

Something about tough times breaks down our boundaries in relationships – on both sides.

Those who normally won't let themselves be helped surrender to support. Those who normally don't want to be pushy feel emboldened to show up and do what needs doing, politeness be damned.

The rawest, most painful and intimate experiences of life (grief, loss, fear, heartbreak, shock) are met with the most potent and powerful resources of humanity (compassion, generosity, kindness, belonging, trust, gratitude). In this way, on our worst days, we actually get to see the best of the people who love us.

Dinners are left on doorsteps. Time is carved out. Beloveds boldly barge in to offer kindness and support when it's needed most. The truth is told, and heard. Pain is witnessed. Notes are written. Strength is shared. We get *together*.

But why do we reserve this only for our tragedies and agonies? Why does it take something tragic to let ourselves be held? Why does it take something agonising for us to drop the facade of etiquette or busyness and just do our best and show up for each other – to really be together?

Let's change that. Let's make a pact: to drop by. To make time. To speak the truth. To listen. To make dinner and leave it on the doorstep. To write a note. To say *I love you*. To hold hands. To not just offer to help, but insist upon it.

Let's make a pact to be our best for each other. Even on the good days.

MAKE LOVE YOUR SKILFUL

STATEMENT

AND YOUR

GRACEFUL RESPONSE

MAKE LOVE YOUR SKILFUL STATEMENT *AND* YOUR GRACEFUL RESPONSE.

E ven if you're a compassionate person, devoted to kindness and cultivating understanding, every so often you probably encounter someone who really gets under your skin. When that happens, remind yourself of this little gem, written by Alan Cohen; it has helped me find compassion for even the most tremendous assholes: 'All acts are expressions of love, either as skillful statements or calls for love in disguised forms.'

Seeing the world through that lens explains a lot, doesn't it? It explains why some people insist on playing the tired old role of martyr or victim. It explains why some people must win at all costs and why kids throw tantrums. It explains overachievement, competitiveness, jealousy, addiction and social media obsession. They're all just calls for love – clumsy, desperate and ugly, perhaps, but calls for love, nonetheless.

The truth is, we all just want to be loved. So let's bring more consciousness to the ways in which we are asking for love. Notice your behaviours and look for opportunities to be a little more honest about what you're really seeking. Look for opportunities to express your love as a skilful statement.

And when you witness an act that is a disguised call for love, choose to see it for what it is. Simply recognising that someone is feeling unloved, outcast, small, alone or disregarded will instantly soften your stance and melt away the armour so that, at the very least, you can meet them with more compassion. At best, you can use the opportunity to respond to their call (however ungainly it may be), rather than rejecting it, thereby breaking a cycle and creating a healed dialogue.

I'm not saying you have to embrace every problematic person in your life, but it helps to remind yourself that we are all seeking the feeling of that four-letter word. See if you can make love both your skilful statement and your graceful response.

COMMITMENT

is the key to freedom

If you want more freedom (more bliss, more spaciousness, more intimacy, more intuition, more reverence, more soul singing, more headspace, more of the things that fill up your cup) it's time to make a commitment.

Discipline and commitment create the conditions for freedom. I'm not talking about diets or strict exercise regimes; I'm talking about making space in your life for the things that light you up. Pay attention to what feels good, and then actively create the conditions for those things to thrive.

Yeah, maybe it's not all sexy and poetic and boho-go-with-the-flow to schedule in a daily meditation, lock in a date night, pencil in fifteen minutes of reading or add a thirty-minute block of creative time to your calendar. But if you genuinely want more of the good stuff, you must invite it into your life by making space for it.

It comes down to intention. When you have a clear intention, you draw up a plan to cultivate it and then you set boundaries in place to protect it, you create the conditions to bring that intention to life. If you say you want to do more writing, dancing, reading, connecting and creating, but then do nothing to invite those things into your daily life, guess what? No dice. Less of the good stuff.

When you choose to create and hold space (even tiny slivers) in your life for the things that give you wings, the rest comes easy. You remove the opportunity for hesitation or hijacking (by things that deem themselves to be more important). There's less chance you'll end up in never-got-around-to-it because you make it happen. Maybe not every day will be a revelation or an epiphany or some great romantic event, but by continually showing up, you invoke a rhythm of creation in your life that seeds more and more of what you want.

Boundaries also illuminate the choices we make. By committing to, say, reading something inspiring for fifteen minutes a day or sitting in meditation for ten minutes every morning, we notice where we might have otherwise mindlessly reached for our phone and got busy scrolling through the 'Gram for twenty minutes (aka a lost opportunity).   >

Commitments open our eyes to the things we say yes to when we really don't mean it: the default 'yes', the accidental 'yes'. The habits, routines and relationships that don't lift us up.

So, pick something that you want more of. Carve out space, make the commitment. Let it be a revolution of small proportions. Start with something manageable: twenty-five minutes, ten minutes, five minutes. Just make it non-negotiable – circle the perimeter like a hawk. Protect what is precious and let it grow.

MORE PLEASURE,

MORE TREASURE

I have good news, y'all: pain is not our only teacher. Pleasure (of the wholesome variety) can *also* light our way and offer meaningful clues. Pain teaches us to muscle our way through. We refer back to our scars as a roadmap, tracing our fingers over these memories as if they are the only way to get through life. And, yes, this can be a seemingly effective way to live. If we've experienced trauma, reflection may even be necessary to our healing. But remember this: pain teaches us how to survive; pleasure shows us how to thrive.

Pain anchors us in the past, pleasure connects us to presence. Pain armours, pleasure reveals. Pleasure teaches us how to surrender – how to move with trust and act intuitively. No pain, no gain? I say: no pleasure, no treasure.

Pleasure reveals our natural inclinations and gifts, and reminds us of what's good and what's easy. While there's a lot to be said about doing what's hard, there's also merit in doing what's easy. Pleasure coaxes us into expansion. It makes us brave, and it lets our souls sing.

Do not hold on to past pain as proof of survival; don't cling to it as if it's a passport to future success. Do not overrate your pain. Do not bind yourself to it. Do not look upon it with indiscriminate pride. Honour your pain, yes. But do not shirk your relationship with pleasure in the name of the perceived bounties and safety of pain. Because pleasure is the way towards thriving.

Let's be clear: when I say *pleasure*, I don't mean smoking a doobie on the couch while you watch the Kardashians and crush an entire tub of Ben & Jerry's. Sorry, love. Numbing doesn't qualify.

Take pleasure in the things that light you up, expand you, deeply relax you and help you settle into yourself, reacquainting you with your true nature. Think brushstrokes of paint on canvas, a dance party in your pjs, dropping lines of poetry onto a blank page, walking in the sun, exchanging pillow talk by candlelight, sipping a hot cup of tea on the front porch, an hour of uninterrupted play with your kids, reading a book made of actual paper, cooking a meal for the fun (not the function) of it, or being of service to others. Those are the real pleasures in life. Those are the pleasures that lead you towards thriving, not just surviving.

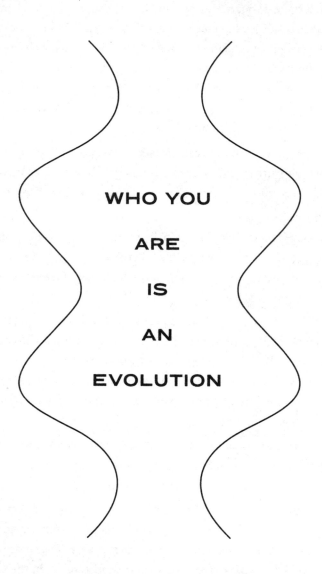

WHO YOU

ARE

IS

AN

EVOLUTION

WHO YOU ARE IS AN EVOLUTION.

Y ou are not bound by contract, fate, inheritance or destiny to live as a fixed version of yourself. You are free: free to change, free to shed your skin, free to walk through a new doorway, free to evolve. You are pure potential. You are limitless. All you need is willingness.

In every moment that you are prepared to step outside of who you think you're supposed to be, you step into your true becoming. You step closer to your true self and you activate your full potential.

Notice any moulds, roles, expectations, obligations, old stories or beliefs that lock you into a fixed state of being. That is not you. That is an expired, outdated idea of you. Who you are is an evolution.

Be willing to give up who you 'are' (who you think you need to be, what someone told you to be or who you used to be) so that you can expand into the limitless potential of your true nature.

Join the evolution revolution. Be willing to become *you*. Over and over again.

VET WHO IS WORTHY OF YOUR VULNERABILITY

I t's hard to be vulnerable. It's uncomfortable to unveil the raw and fragile aspects of ourselves. It's hard to show how much it hurts, how scared we are, how lost or lonely we feel. It's uncomfortable to lay out our pain, piece by piece. Sharing our failings, fears and (so-called) flaws can feel like taking a public inventory of our most intimate experiences. It can leave us feeling exposed and unguarded – worse than if we'd just kept quiet.

It's true that some people will betray the sacredness of your trust and vulnerability. Some people will use your pain as fodder for gossip. Some people will use it as a way to make themselves feel superior. Some people will betray your vulnerability by simply not grasping the gravity of what you've shared. And that hurts, too.

One option to avoid all of this is to build a big f*cking wall. Let no one in. Lock that shit down. Keep quiet. This can feel like the safest option. It's consistent and easy to stick to – a policy of total privacy. But it's also a recipe for accumulating and storing experiences somatically, packing our cells with unprocessed emotions that have been poisoned by the shame of being made unspeakable.

This kind of emotional vigilance also isolates us, preventing us from creating any kind of true intimacy with others – which means we miss out on closeness, connection, community, collective problem-solving, healing, belonging and joy. These things make the human experience magical, but they require vulnerability and trust.

So here's my suggestion: be vulnerable *sometimes*. The truth is that some people are deserving of your trust and vulnerability. And some people are just ... not. That's okay.

Vulnerability works best and achieves its highest aims (connecting us and helping us heal) when it is met with respect and reverence. So don't shut down. Be brave enough to be vulnerable, but be discerning. Vet who is worthy of your vulnerability. Then share accordingly.

GET OUT OF YOUR HEAD

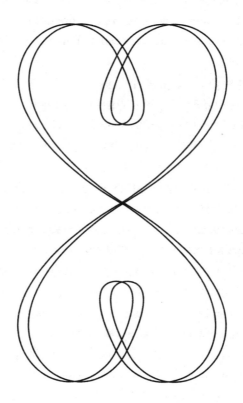

AND INTO YOUR HEART

GET OUT OF YOUR HEAD AND INTO YOUR HEART.

F ear and courage are steady companions, but only one can be in charge at a time. So who is running your life most of the time? Your head or your heart?

Don't get me wrong – the mind is very useful for weighing and measuring, charting a path and carving the soft and atmospheric visions of the heart into something refined and real. But take care not to let the mind bully your heart into stunned submission.

Don't let the paranoid rampaging of the mind trample the goodness, wonder and hope in your heart.

The mind is welcome for its insights and protective directives, but it should never be given the power to veto the truth in your heart.

Because the heart – not the mind – is the seat of courage and the speaker of the soul. You attune to the mission of your soul not by submitting to every brassy, bossy thought issued by the mind, but by carefully heeding the low, soft guidance of your heart.

Your heart, even now, beats out the steady anthem of your soul, cheering you on. So get out of your head and into your heart.

Live from that place. Dance to that beat. Listen to the wise counsel of your cells, singing their resonance or rejection. Trust yourself. Dance this life to your heartbeat.

let go of your story, start living your life.

A re you tired of that same old story? You know, the one where you're the loud one, the stupid one, the perfect one, the funny one, the smart one, the popular one, the lonely one or the responsible one? Your story might be about your romantic relationships, your work life, your personality, your body or your family. Or maybe you're re-learning the same lesson again and again, repeating patterns or cycles or hearing yourself saying the same words day in and day out? Your story could be about overwhelm or loneliness, boldness or meekness, betrayal or bitterness, loss or loathing.

All of us have stories we've been saddled with. The stories might be yours – a series of narratives you've constructed. Or they might be a collection of tales someone told you about yourself many years ago that you've adopted and taken as truth – pieces of feedback from a teacher, parent or lover that you're 'too this' or 'too that'.

Even a well-meaning compliment can feel like a life sentence. If you've let yourself be branded in a particular way, you'll feel committed to that character, till death do you part.

Here's the thing: the stories we tell ourselves *about* ourselves become the scripts for our lives. That's why the story you're telling yourself matters. Who you are is an evolution, so if you're tuning in to the same old tale, year after year, you're stunting your growth.

The truth is, most of these stories are works of fiction – misremembered history or hyperbole masquerading as facts. But you're not stuck with your story; it's not set in stone. Don't let yourself be held captive by some BS story, playing a role you didn't choose for yourself. Don't believe yourself to be shipwrecked, stranded with some tale you were told about yourself. Don't cling to your story as if it were your only hope for the future. Your history is not a prophecy.

If your inner narrator is stuck on repeat, you have a choice: keep listening to the same story or write a new one. Rip out the old pages and burn them to ash. Start with a blank page and write it from scratch. Make it an epic adventure. Make it a saga of sweetness. Make it a creative crusade. Make it a heart-thumping romance. Make it an inner expedition, pioneering uncharted territories. Make it a story of courage and bravery. >

Make it a legend of love. Make it a quest for truth. Whatever story you write about yourself, make it your own. Make it on purpose.

Put down the old script. Pick up a pencil. It's time to let go of your story and start living your life.

BE AN

imperfectionist

BE AN IMPERFECTIONIST.

I 've learned that death changes your relationship with fear. Unexpectedly losing someone you love can make you feel intensely anxious and controlling. (You don't want to let anyone you love out of your sight ... ever again.) And yet, loss also makes you brave as hell. You realise just how precious this life is, how uncertain your time here is and how the judgements of others you fear so much matter so little.

You come to understand how much you have to lose (your beloveds). Paradoxically, you also realise how much you have to give – and how little you have to lose by being brave and generous with your life, instead of worrying about whether you're good enough.

I'm not afraid of being imperfect anymore. I'm not afraid of not being good enough. I'm more afraid of dying with all this goodness stuck inside of me, unused and unshared. When it's my time to go, I want to know in my bones that I didn't let fear get in the way of sharing my gifts. I don't want to live a small, perfect life – I want to live a big, brave, imperfect one. Are you with me? Don't waste a moment of this life, my love!

If you're waiting until your plate isn't so full, your to-do list is done, your laundry is all folded, your closet is cleaned out, your dishes are done, your hamstrings are more flexible, your mind is more still, your body is slimmer, your poem is more finished or your prototype is more polished ... stop.

Stop being a perfectionist. Stop waiting for everything to be in perfect order. Stop waiting for the perfect time. Stop waiting for the clean slate. Stop hiding behind order and control. Stop second-guessing. Stop procrastinating away this life you have to live, the goodness you can give and all the joy there is for you to have. Stop waiting to be perfect.

Instead, just start. Start now, just as you are, just as your life is. Tight hamstrings, busy mind, full schedule, shoestring budget, basketfuls of laundry, sink full of dishes, paintings that could use just one more stroke, poems that could use one less word, ideas that could be more polished, timing that could be better.

F*ck it. Get out there and live. >

Start doing the things you've been meaning to do. Start writing, start painting, start meditating, start stretching, sign up for the course, send the proposal, book the ticket, post the poem, share the photo, mail the letter, read the book, make time for the friend, have the party, speak up, sing, pack the picnic, lie on your back underneath the stars – and laugh while the dishes fill the sink and the laundry sits undone.

Because that is living.

Perfectionism steals your life. Imperfection lets you do more livin'. So start living like an imperfectionist. Being fully alive looks good on you, and living your life fully means we all get to delight in the goodness that you have to share.

make a date with *delight*

We are so focused on outputs and production and perfection. We are driven by what needs to get done – by function, by outcomes, by what can be measured. We tick boxes and do reps. We look at things critically and analytically. We spend our time 'wisely', by which we (rather ironically) mean 'productively': working, exercising, cooking, cleaning, repeating – constantly pursuing productivity.

It's true that some of these tasks may have a side effect of enjoyment (the home chef who loves cooking, the writer who loves writing, the body that loves moving). But mostly we concern ourselves with functional activity. We are seldom purely in pursuit of pleasure.

But at the end of the day, at the end of the year, at the end of this life, what will you reflect on? Are memories and meaning made and measured in moments of productivity? Or, rather, do they rise out of those rare pockets of pleasure and presence in our lives? The moments when we just ... let ourselves have the moment? The occasions when we slow down enough to notice the subtle ecstasy of the everyday?

Think about the slow mornings in bed. The bowl of freshly cooked food eaten on the grass. Just-cut gardenias. The unhurried moment. Tea drunk hot. Dog-eared pages. Kitchen table conversations. Handwritten notes. Silk or sunshine or sea water on skin. A spoonful of honey. Laughter in the dark.

I, for one, don't want delight, beauty, pleasure and presence to be afterthoughts or side effects in my life. I refuse to make order, productivity and outputs the measures of my life.

I believe that delight is evidence of the divine. I want to make space in my life for that grace. I want to be in conversation with joy. I want to make a regular date with delight. Will you join me?

What would that look like for you? To open yourself to something purely for the pleasure of it? What if pleasure was your priority? What if joy was your first concern? What if you were incited by delight? What joy would you find? What gratification awaits you if you give yourself permission to truly delight in your life? How much more satisfying might life be? >

Let's find out the answers to those questions, shall we? Here's the invitation: make a date with delight. Invite it into your life.

Delight is defined as 'a high degree of pleasure or enjoyment; joy; rapture' or 'to give great pleasure, satisfaction or enjoyment to; to please highly'. So let yourself do something totally delightful each day – even if only for ten minutes. Something highly, purely pleasurable, and absolutely, unapologetically unproductive.

Bonus: document your delights! Just as you might start your day with a gratitude journal, you can end your day by noting down the day's delights. A simple sentence scribbled in your journal is enough to chronicle your dalliances with delight. And the more you notice what delights you, the more you celebrate it. The more you become attuned to the (otherwise missed) opportunities for delight in your day. Delight becomes a daily practice, which adds up to a more delightful life. Enjoy.

RISE ABOVE THE *resistance.* FIND THE COURAGE TO *commit.*

RISE ABOVE THE RESISTANCE.
FIND THE COURAGE TO COMMIT.

It's time to commit – to your dreams, your goals, your desires. Stop waiting for someone to tell you which way to turn. Stop hesitating. Stop ruminating. Stop second-guessing. Stop letting self-doubt drag you back. Stop waiting for the right time or the right sign. Stop wondering about what could be and *go find out*.

The resistance you're feeling may be strong, but it's wrong. Resistance tells you it's keeping you safe, but it's really keeping you small.

Think about what's worse: trying (and maybe not succeeding) or living with the regret that you never even tried. The biggest failure isn't the person who gives it a shot and flops. The biggest failure is the person who never tries.

So screw the resistance and f*ck that fear of failure. Of course you can't control the outcomes, but you can decide if your dreams matter enough to try. Every day you are either drifting away from your dreams or charging towards them. What are you going to do today? Are you going to take steps forwards or backwards? It's your choice.

My advice (to us all): rise above the din of resistance. Choose your potential. Find the courage to commit. Lace up your boots. Pick up your tools. Start moving. It's time.

LET YOUR LIFE BE AN EXULTATION, NOT AN EXERCISE IN STAYING SAFE

LET YOUR LIFE BE AN EXULTATION, NOT AN EXERCISE IN STAYING SAFE.

A s humans, we're primed to look for what's wrong. We're wired to be on alert. To be fair, vigilance has been a useful tool, inherent to our evolutionary success. But when you add trauma to our predilection for overcaution, the fear can code a pattern of suffering, shame and contraction into our cells.

Frozen in hypervigilance, we could easily spend our entire lives in perpetual anticipation of pain and suffering, worrying ourselves sick. It's a well-worn path in our modern bodies and we travel it with familiarity.

Strangely, worrying can feel like an insurance policy – if we're constantly on alert to all of the possible threats and potential for suffering (the worst-case scenarios), it somehow makes us feel safer. So our minds become fear-mongering fortune tellers, consumed with estimating, measuring and calculating potential threats – physical, emotional and otherwise.

There's a limit to the usefulness of all this vigilance.

Vigilance tears us away from presence, which is the seat of contentment and satisfaction. It anaesthetises our intuition, making us deaf to the truth of our insight and self-knowledge, leaving us stripped of self-trust and unable to wisely guide ourselves through our lives. It shuts off the stream of joy that otherwise flows through us. It contracts our attention, making us blind to the bliss that's right in front of us.

The truth is, it's damn near impossible to feel happy when you're perpetually worried about what's around the corner.

So don't let vigilance steal your joy. Don't miss the bliss. Don't forfeit your birthright of delight, wonder and rapture. Here's the good news: your joy is intact. It is waiting for you, unchanging. You just need to awaken yourself to it, bit by bit.

Reclaim your joy. Scratch away the layers of fear that are keeping you separate from your truth. (Bonus: turning up the dial on joy dims the reflex of hypervigilance.) Start with a breath, a list of what you're grateful for, a pocket of pleasure, a steaming hot bath, a cup of tea in the sunshine, a belly laugh with your babe. Pay attention to the positive. >

When vigilance creeps in, diffuse it with these questions: 'Is this true? Is this useful? Where am I choosing to put my focus in this moment?' Where possible, swap your fearful thoughts with loving ones. Replace fear with love over and over again and it becomes your default.

Savour this life, sweet one. Treasure the endowment of the pleasure and bliss that is yours. Let your life be an exultation, not an exercise in staying safe.

You're not stuck.

Your thoughts are.

Your thoughts are.

You're not stuck.

YOU'RE NOT STUCK. YOUR THOUGHTS ARE.

Repetitive, negative thoughts are thoughts that are stuck in the past. They have nothing new to offer. There is no fresh wisdom, no golden instruction, no promises of potential. Old, stuck thoughts carry the tones of shame and sorrow. They do not sing up our souls, conjuring the best of us. They do not give us a blueprint for doing better. Old thoughts just keep us feeling stuck.

But here's the thing: you already got the message, probably five thousand times by now. You. Got. It. So why are you listening to the same old shit?

Here's an invitation: if your inner DJ is stuck on repeat with some tired old track about *not enough* (not enough time, not enough money, not enough talent, or that you yourself are simply not good enough), *pick up the needle*. Choose another track. Tune in to the voice of change, not the voice of shame. (Note: they are not the same.)

Where do you want to go? Place your thoughts ahead of you. Be forward thinking. Your thoughts are creative. They can help you craft your future reality. So create something new. Listen to something that makes you *move*, not something that keeps you stuck.

Turn up the volume on the soundtrack to your soul. Come on, baby! You've got this one life. Dance to the beat of your full potential, not your supposed shortcomings. Move to the music of your magnificence. You are divine, you are literally miraculous, you are a creation of the cosmos.

So think like it.

SELF-FORGIVENESS IS AN ACT OF REBELLION.

SELF-FORGIVENESS IS AN ACT OF REBELLION.

SELF-FORGIVENESS IS AN ACT OF REBELLION.

SELF-FORGIVENESS IS AN ACT OF REBELLION.

SELF-FORGIVENESS IS AN ACT OF REBELLION.

SELF-FORGIVENESS IS AN ACT OF REBELLION.

SELF-FORGIVENESS IS AN ACT OF REBELLION.

SELF-FORGIVENESS IS AN ACT OF REBELLION.

SELF-FORGIVENESS IS AN ACT OF REBELLION.

SELF-FORGIVENESS IS AN ACT OF REBELLION.

SELF-FORGIVENESS IS AN ACT OF REBELLION.

SELF-FORGIVENESS IS AN ACT OF REBELLION.

SELF-FORGIVENESS IS AN ACT OF REBELLION.

SELF-FORGIVENESS IS AN ACT OF REBELLION.

SELF-FORGIVENESS IS AN ACT OF REBELLION.

SELF-FORGIVENESS IS AN ACT OF REBELLION.

SELF-FORGIVENESS IS AN ACT OF REBELLION.

If you're carrying the weight of guilt or shame, if you're feeling powerless or paralysed, it's time to shed the shame and honour the goodness within you that wants to do well.

It's time to create a revolution for radical kindness in your heart. Because self-forgiveness gives you permission to evolve and to continually become your very best self.

Self-forgiveness is a rebellion against the misery of perfectionism.

Self-forgiveness is the reclamation of your agency over your life: your power and your freedom.

Self-forgiveness resolves you to a new perspective and a fresh start.

And the more readily you are able to forgive yourself, the more compassion, forgiveness and kindness you can extend to others.

So start a revolution in your heart with these three words: *I forgive myself.* Forgive yourself for whatever you've done or haven't done, whatever your perceived failures or shortcomings, however many missteps or misspoken words you've collected. You are always deserving of your own forgiveness, and self-forgiveness is the path back to wholeness.

Remember that this life is a practice: of coming home to ourselves, of forgiving ourselves, of blessing ourselves and each other. Over and over again.

YOUR FUTURE AIN'T WHAT IT USED TO BE

YOUR FUTURE AIN'T WHAT IT USED TO BE.

I s your orientation towards your history or your destiny? Do you have a loyalty to your past or to your future? Are you reliving, retelling and reinforcing a well-worn, recycled story? Are you doing things in the same old way? Are you using the past as proof of what the future holds?

Or are you daring to do it differently by dreaming up a new way forwards? Because the choice is always yours: keep recollecting and stay in the past, or forecast a fresh future for yourself.

Here's the good news: you don't owe your old ideas anything. It doesn't matter who you thought you loved, what you thought was right or where you thought you'd be. So shed the old beliefs that no longer serve you. Drop the stories about why it didn't work or how you got it wrong.

Say 'peace out' to the past. Put a fresh face forwards. Dare to do it differently. Dance with your destiny, because the truth is that destiny trumps history.

And your future ain't what it used to be.

SPEND YOUR INNER
RESOURCES WISELY

SPEND YOUR INNER RESOURCES WISELY.

A re the most important things in your life getting leftovers? Are the people and passions that matter most being treated as an afterthought?

Do you choose to scrub your toilet or fold towels instead of building cubby houses with your kids? Do you work so much and so hard that you have no time or energy to give your loved ones at the end of the day? Do you tell yourself you're too busy with work to take a holiday with your family or go to your friend's wedding?

Do you give most of your attention to the customer who complains, or to the customer who is loyal and devoted? Did you have time to post on Instagram but felt you were too busy to text back your bestie?

Do you run out of time to meditate in the morning because you woke up and scrolled through your socials first thing? Do you sit down with a clear mind and fresh ideas, but then clear your inbox, pay some bills and do a bit of online shopping instead of writing the story that's waiting inside of you?

Do you watch TV instead of throwing down a drop cloth and pulling out your palette and paintbrushes? Do you stare at your screen at night, scrolling through photos of people you don't know instead of looking into the eyes of someone who matters deeply?

Your attention, time and energy are currency. Where are you spending them? Where are you investing your most precious resources?

Ask yourself what matters most to you. And then consider this: are your actions moving you towards or away from what (or who) matters most?

Spend your inner resources wisely, my friend.

RESPECT + PROTECT YOUR BOUNDARIES
RESPECT + PROTECT YOUR BOUNDARIES
RESPECT + PROTECT YOUR BOUNDARIES
RESPECT + PROTECT YOUR BOUNDARIES
RESPECT + PROTECT YOUR BOUNDARIES
RESPECT + PROTECT YOUR BOUNDARIES
RESPECT + PROTECT YOUR BOUNDARIES
RESPECT + PROTECT YOUR BOUNDARIES

G et home from work totally tapped out and irritated because you carried the load for your co-workers? Have a houseful of guests and feel like you got hit by a truck? Regularly bump all of your priorities to the bottom of the list so you can help someone else – and then feel annoyed with yourself? Busy making everyone else comfortable at the expense of your own comfort? Showing up to help and then feeling angry in the aftermath? You, my friend, may have boundary issues.

My friend, Dr Scott Lyons, once told me that anger is the signal that lets us know our boundaries have been crossed. Note that anger is not synonymous with rage. Yes, anger can be heated – like when you want to flip the bird or throw a plate at the wall. But anger has a lot of other, less fiery flavours like feeling annoyed, frustrated, hurt, overwhelmed, scared, or having a sense of unfairness and injustice about a situation.

In this way, the many faces of anger are all just trying to point out to you that a line has been crossed. They're sounding an alarm to say, 'Hey, honey, someone's all up in your shit.' So instead of shaming your feelings, thank them for the service they provide – protecting your boundaries.

Here's the thing: boundaries are, in essence, about self-respect. Boundaries require you to value yourself enough to respect and protect your inner resources, to be a good steward of your gifts, your time and your energy. Boundaries ask you to know your limits and honour them with integrity.

True, laying out boundaries takes bravery and confidence. But people won't like you less or think you're crazy for having boundaries. In fact, people will probably respect you more. And they'll be more than willing to respect your boundaries if they know where they are.

On that note, don't assume that people know where your boundaries are or that they have the same tolerance as you. Don't assume others know better. Some people are blind to boundaries and need a little extra guidance. But most people will happily stay on their side, if you show them where the line is. So show them. Make it clear – for both of you.

Survey your territory and claim your domain. Draw a circle around it. Protect your boundaries gently or fiercely, whatever is called for.   >

But protect them proudly. Do not let every customer, family member or friend hopscotch across your borders without your permission. Be brave enough to respect and protect your boundaries. Patrol your borders like a foot soldier, marching with integrity and purpose. Meet those who attempt to transgress with firmness, but also kindness. And when your feelings sound the alarm that a boundary has been violated, retrace the line, carve it out a little more clearly and begin again.

YOU ARE THE

BOSS

OF YOUR VIBE

YOU ARE THE BOSS OF YOUR VIBE.

A s a little girl, my first phrase was, 'You're not the boss of me, I'm the boss of me.'

I stand by those words – not just when I want to have cake for break-fast, but also when it's time to hold myself accountable. I recognise that I'm in charge of my vibe. No one else is responsible for the bad habits or sloppy self-care that can lead to low vibes. I'm the boss of me. So when my headspace heads south, I know who to turn to: *myself*.

You probably know the things that work well for you: the habits and rituals that help you shine. It's just a matter of coming home to them. Of recommitting to the relationship between yourself and the things that serve you, not the things that tear you down, deplete you or kill your mood.

If you can relate, if you've slipped or spiralled or been a little sloppy, consider this your invitation. Start today. Remember that you are the one and only boss of your vibe. Clean up your act. Reorient to your high-est self. Draw boundaries around the things that f*ck with your focus, knock you out of alignment or make you feel cramped, sad, frustrated or overwhelmed. Recommit to the things that make you feel good – the habits and rituals that make you feel spacious, focused, positive and aligned with what matters most to you and how you want to show up in the world. Reclaim your agency. Give yourself some marching orders that will make you shine, not shrink. 'Cause you're the boss, boo.

you don't need a plan

I have great news: you don't have to know what you want to 'do with your life'. Or who you're going to be 'when you grow up'. You don't need a five-year plan or a resumé that 'makes sense'. You don't need to forecast your life. You don't need to figure it all out. You just need to keep iterating.

Iteration is the circular rhythm of evolution: experimentation, reflection and refinement, repeated as often as necessary. This repetition forms the process of personal evolution (your becoming) that is the path to those full-potential feels of freedom, fulfilment and joy. Planning can't give you those feelings, but iterating can.

Because remember: your full potential isn't a destination somewhere in the future. The opportunity to live to your full potential is now. Right now, in each moment. In each iteration.

When you give yourself permission to iterate, you free yourself from the paralysis of perfectionism and the idea that you need to figure it out *first*. Instead, you get to try it out *now* and figure out a better way *next*.

Iteration is an invitation to follow your instincts, to experiment, to take risks, to be playful, to explore the edges of yourself. To see what's possible, and upgrade as you go. Through iteration, you free yourself from the debt of regret – because there are no regrets in experimentation, just discoveries. Your next step can never be a misstep if it's an iteration. An iteration can never be a failure, because failure is married to finality – and only death is final. So, in my book, if you're iterating you're succeeding. Because you're out here, really livin', kid.

There's no award for who figured their shit out first, who had the best plan, who held their job longest or who met their soulmate soonest. There's no need to freak out about what you want to do with your life or where you're going to end up. Just figure out what you're going to do *next*. Then get out there and f*cking *iterate*.

Take things down to parts. Rebuild. Fall in love. Say goodbye. Have a good idea and change your mind. Buy. Sell. Make something. Keep what works. Make another version. Throw out the batch. Rinse the bowl. Begin again. Try the thing. Tweak it. Pivot. Make it better. Pay attention. Keep going. Experiment. Reflect. Refine. Repeat.

Planning is overrated. Iteration is where it's at.

LOVE

YOURSELF

FIERCELY

LOVE YOURSELF FIERCELY.

So much of the way we speak to ourselves and about ourselves, and the way we move, eat and care for ourselves physically and emotionally, is out of habit. A habit is a stubborn neurological pattern. It's a set of well-worn tracks that the wagon wheels of our behaviour sink into effortlessly.

How you treat yourself matters. It sets a standard for how you expect others to treat you. By being in a loving and kind relationship with yourself, you're inviting the other relationships in your life to also be loving and kind.

So take a little inventory of how well you are loving yourself. If your relationship with yourself could use a little upgrade, start now. Notice your internal dialogue and choose a different tone if it's less than loving.

Be your own biggest advocate, your number-one fan, your BFF. Speak to and of yourself as you would a beloved child – with nourishing, kind, compassionate and encouraging words.

Feel grateful when you move your body. Take in the landscape of your body like a lover would: a field of sensation to be celebrated. Regard your body not as a burden, but as a precious vessel you've been entrusted with. Honour it and nourish it with care and attention and choices that say 'I love you and I am deeply grateful.'

Treat yourself to something that fills you with delight. A catnap, a hot bath, a walk on the beach, a foot massage, a phone call with a friend who makes you laugh, a juicy meditation, an early night tucked in bed. Whatever makes your heart open up. Gift it to yourself.

You are worthy of love – especially your own. So go ahead and love yourself fiercely. Lead by example. Show the world how it's done.

being wrong *is* alright

BEING WRONG IS ALRIGHT.

W rongness is something we seem to dodge at all costs. We make an excuse, create a justification, redirect the responsibility to someone else or even flat out lie. We associate wrongness with the pain of imperfection. We're afraid of being wrong because we mistake it for failure.

But that's where we get it, well, wrong. Making mistakes and being wrong aren't a disadvantage. Quite the opposite. In fact, hiding from our wrongness is missing an opportunity, because all our opportunities to learn, grow and change rest in our willingness to be wrong.

When we own the fact that we don't know the answer, made the wrong move or said the wrong thing, or even just admit that there might be another way, we create an opportunity for learning and growth.

If you never admit you don't know, how can you ever learn more? If you never do it the wrong way, how will you figure out the right way? If you never break the thing, how will you discover how to build it better?

So stop hiding from being wrong. Being wrong is alright. In fact, admitting we're wrong activates our righteousness through the grace of curiosity. Curiosity helps us see things with fresh eyes, find solutions, create a better way, innovate, improve and – maybe most importantly – seek unity. (Curiosity and empathy go hand in hand, after all.)

Curiosity unveils the path towards healing, learning, growth and improvement – also known as the road to being right. So stop fearing wrongness and start inviting it. Be teachable. Be curious. Be willing to be wrong. Because being wrong is alright.

FOLDED WINGS WON'T HELP YOU FLY

FOLDED WINGS WON'T HELP YOU FLY.

I know you have secrets, baby: those dreams you have that are so bold you dare not speak them. That vision for your life that is so vast and so bright you can only squint in its direction.

Those dreams and visions offer a peek at your potential. So why are you keeping them secret? Why are you superstitiously guarding them?

I'll tell you why: fear. Because what if you fail? The (misplaced) shame of potential failure keeps you frozen on the spot, or only inching towards your full potential. You're walking tentatively like a bird built for flight, afraid to spread its wings, ineffectually picking its way forwards, eyes on the ground, heading nowhere far and nowhere fast.

Here's the thing: you, dear one, were designed to fly.

So if you've been picking your way forwards on foot, wings clasped close to your body, hear this: folded wings won't help you fly.

Unconfine yourself. Trust in your inborn buoyancy. Unfold those wings. Feel their width, then leap.

Each wingbeat is the pulse of your purpose, thrusting you forwards towards your full potential. It takes courage to fly, yes, but your soul is streamlined to slip through resistance and keep you soaring ever onwards, ever forwards, ever upwards.

Go. Spread those wings. It's time to fly. Your dreams are waiting for you.

~~Get through it~~

Grow through it

L osses, tough breaks, failure, sorrow, grief and sadness are all part of this human experience. And though we may not be able to control what are often the most difficult circumstances in our life, we *can* control how we relate to them.

One option is to shrink: to be brittle, to slump, to shrink, to plod forwards, to get through it.

Or you can stretch yourself: forge new tools, expand your capacity for life. *Grow* through it.

The truth is that every challenge in your life is an opportunity for growth. Every hardship, every heartbreak, every uphill battle, every burden, every stressor, every misfortune, every tragedy, every trauma and every unhappiness is a call for expansion. Difficulty is an invitation to increase your capacity – for grace, for resilience, for gratitude, for compassion, for understanding, for life.

Think about it: the greatest periods of growth in your life were probably garnered from challenging experiences. Every challenge stretches you (if you're flexible and willing) into the next version of yourself: your bigger self, your higher self.

So, rather than buckling under the weight of your hardships, how can you rise up to meet them? How can you show up for what life is asking of you? How can you be courageous? How can you spiral outward and explore the edges of your capacity? How can you remember just how big and capable you really are? How can you keep *growing* through challenges rather than just *going* through them? How can you ace this assignment in the curriculum of your life?

And if you're wondering 'Why bother?', here's why: your contraction serves no one. Your expansion serves the world. A more compassionate, more humble, more grateful, more resilient human is a gift to us all.

So remember, when shit hits the fan it's a call to expand. Heed the call. Be courageous. Be flexible. Be willing. Show up. Rise up. Stretch. Shine.

Don't just get through life. Grow through it.

BE IN
PURSUIT
OF
LESS

As a culture, we're pretty obsessed with more. More food. More friends (or, ahem, more followers). Doing more work so we can get more things. Filling our closets to the brim, jamming up our inboxes with sale emails, packing our days with more than we can actually get done, setting more goals without thinking about why and padding our calendars with friendships that are more filler than fun. We are full steam ahead in pursuit of more.

And, to be fair, it's easy to get caught up in the momentum of more. That's the dream we've been sold; it's marketed to us every day. We're accumulation ninjas, trained in excess, experts at avoiding emptiness.

But if we keep filling up our bellies and our closets and our calendars, we don't have time to understand what emptiness feels like – or what it can offer us.

Emptiness brings us face to face with uncertainty, vulnerability and even loneliness. Emptiness asks us tough questions, like 'What do you really, really want?' and 'Who are you, really?' These questions are hard to answer because, in becoming expert consumers and accumulators, we've numbed our sense of discernment. We've lost the ability to define what our style is, what we're hungry for, what kinds of friends we want and what we desire. We can't decide what we actually want or need.

So maybe what we really need is *less*. The truth is that less can actually feel like freedom, focus and clarity. There is nothing to distract, muddy or cover over the essence of you, your feelings, your desires or your truth.

What if we spent a little time untangling ourselves from the web of excess, pulling out the weeds to make more room for the things we truly love to take root and bloom? What if we devoted ourselves to clarifying and intentionally cultivating?

I'm not saying you should go and live in an ashram (unless ashrams are your happy place, in which case, go for it!). But you should define your desires and let your desires define your choices. That starts with flinging open the doors and going in pursuit of less – so you can gain more of what *really* matters.　　　　　　　　　　　　　　>

Less stuff. More space.

Less doing. More being.

Less trying. More trusting.

Less speed. More soul.

Less mindlessness. More mindfulness.

Less focus on making a profit. More focus on making a difference.

Less striving. More serving.

Less control. More trust.

Less aggression. More grace.

Less perfection. More authenticity.

Heck, less toast. More *jam*.

The way I see it, *less* can actually be a luxury.

shift
happens

J ust when the caterpillar thought the world was over, it became a butterfly. It's cutesy and clichéd, but it's also true. On our path of growth, we sometimes have to die a small death to live a bigger life.

We get hung up on wanting to be in a perpetual state of expansion, but that's not how it works, folks. Linear growth is a myth. Evolution isn't a smooth, upward curve; it's a pulse, a wave, a heartbeat. You are designed to contract and expand. Contraction followed by expansion is, in fact, the most fundamental rhythm of life.

Shapeshifting (catharsis, growth, change – call it what you will) demands that we experience a contraction before we expand into our next expression. It asks that we wade through sweat and tears. It strips us down to our most vulnerable, raw self. It sometimes requires us to totally lose our bearings. But most of all, shifting asks us to bear witness to the transition with total willingness.

When you let go of the attachment to expansion and stop fighting the contraction, you surrender to the rhythm of your evolution.

Surrender doesn't mean letting the process happen to you like you're a helpless, rubbernecking bystander to your life. Surrendering means embracing the contraction (the breakdown, the shrinking, the resting, the self-doubt) with your whole self so that when the time for expansion comes (and it *always* does) you can unfold those prized, well-earned wings and fly free.

Just as the ocean draws herself back before thrusting her full force magnificently upon the shore, you too must recede and regather yourself before bursting forth once more.

This is transformation. This is growth. This is the process of expansion. First: you get small. Then: you get bigger. Contraction, expansion. Drawing in, breaking through. Shrinking, shining.

So if life is feeling stuck or shitty or small right now, stop fighting it. Surrender to the process. Yes, it's messy and uncomfortable and uncertain. But it's *right*. You are incubating another, higher incarnation of your truest self. You are unfolding. You are growing. You are shifting. It *is* happening. The answers are coming. Shift happens.

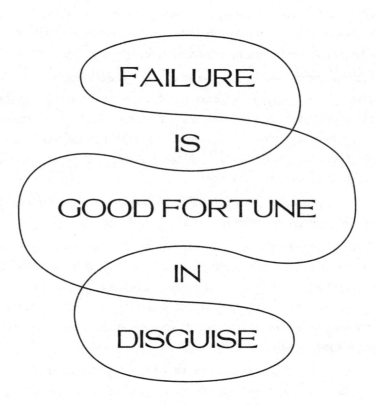

FAILURE IS GOOD FORTUNE IN DISGUISE

FAILURE IS GOOD FORTUNE IN DISGUISE.

What if failure isn't failure, but a gift? What if failure is your teacher, instructing you on what is not for you, what not to do, who not to be, who not to be with?

What if failure is an opportunity? What if failure is freedom? What if you celebrated your failures rather than dismissing or hiding them? What if every failure was just guiding you to course-correct and return to the slipstream of your soul? What if failure was redirecting you to use your unique gifts in the most useful way possible?

What would it feel like to relieve yourself of the burden of failure? What would it feel like to say thank you to the projects, ideas, plans and relationships that have failed? 'Thank you for failing so that I can return to what works. Thank you for failing so that, next time, I'll know better. Thank you for failing because I am now crystal clear on what I do want, and what I don't want. Thank you for failing so that I can be free. Thank you for failing so that I can find my way to what is meant for me.'

Maybe we should stop fearing failure so much. Because maybe failure is just good fortune in disguise.

CELEBRATE COMMON GROUND
CELEBRATE COMMON GROUND
CELEBRATE COMMON GROUND
CELEBRATE COMMON GROUND
CELEBRATE COMMON GROUND
CELEBRATE COMMON GROUND
CELEBRATE COMMON GROUND
CELEBRATE COMMON GROUND

P olarised perspectives and critical thinking come naturally to us as humans. We're wired to look for threats and defend ourselves. Our ego defines itself by what it is *not*. We're comfortable living in black and white: us and them, wrong and right, yes and no. We lean into conflict and our opinions become razor sharp, cutting through connections so that 'clear' lines are drawn.

No doubt there are plenty of things to take a stand against these days. I'm all for opinions and using our voices, but sometimes we disagree as a reflex and respond without even listening.

We spend a great deal of energy creating division in our lives. But, please, be discerning. Be careful that you don't become so firmly rooted in your own opinions and perspectives that you alienate yourself from curiosity and open exchange. Because the truth is, if we want the world to change, we need to start conversations, not end them.

So check in with yourself: how much of your day do you spend in resistance, disagreement or opposition? How much of your time do you spend looking for what's wrong, criticising, correcting or countering? Is disagreeing a reflex? Is defence your first reaction?

What if we did a little experiment and took a holiday, for an hour or a day, from the posturing and opposition? What if we listened more? What if we seized opportunities to unite rather than divide? What if we gave the benefit of the doubt a little more often? What if we softened the blades of our opinions? What if we took things less personally? What if we asked more questions? What if we laughed a little more? What if we noticed what we have in common – and celebrated it?

Sift through the moments of your day and ask yourself whether there are occasions to say these words more often: 'Yes' or 'I agree' or 'Go on ...' or 'Tell me more'. Are there opportunities to offer a compliment instead of pumping out criticism? Are there times when you could listen with a little more curiosity and compassion and a little less jumping to conclusions? Could you fling open the door instead of defending the fort?

Try it and see what happens. You might be surprised by how much commonality and connection is there when you lean in and listen gently and generously. It's a harder path, but one that leads to higher ground.

DON'T LET SUNK COSTS SINK YOU

W hether it's a floundering business, an idea that flopped, an unproductive investment, a dwindling romance, a losing bet, a pear-shaped partnership or an unpublished manuscript, losing the sunk costs of money, time and energy that (apparently) produced no fruit can feel like a kick in the guts.

Sometimes that pain is so great and we're so embarrassed to admit our big idea didn't work that we're afraid of walking away from those sunk costs. So we keep throwing in good money (or time, or love), freezing ourselves in a failing situation. Or we become petrified of making another move, fearful of ever investing time or money again because we've given ourselves a vote of no confidence. We think, 'Well, shit. That didn't go to plan. So I can't be trusted.'

Either way, we're stuck: stuck in a failing situation, or stuck in the fear of future failure.

But sunk costs don't have to sink you.

Here's a reframe worth making: you didn't lose anything. It wasn't a loss at all; it was a gain.

Anytime you thoroughly fail, you earn yourself a degree. The money you paid, the time you spent, the energy you invested – that's all just tuition paid to the School of Life. It's an investment in your education.

You gained knowledge and know-how. You gained experience. You gained insight. Your eyes have been trained to see things in new ways. Maybe you learned a new skill in the process. Maybe you learned a life lesson. Maybe there was an unexpected silver lining or a hidden gem – something you learned about yourself, an uncovered passion. Maybe the failure actually paved the way towards long-term success by leading you to something you couldn't have imagined before. Maybe you're more discerning about who to trust with your ideas, money or time. Maybe you know better *now*, so you can do better *next*.

So don't get hung up on a number being in the red, or a partnership that wasn't the big-picture solution you thought it would be, or a book that needs to be rewritten, or a million-dollar idea that didn't add up to anything, or an investment that went wobbly and capsized. It's just the price you paid for the skills and wisdom you got in exchange. >

As long as you take notes and use those earned assets in whatever comes next, it's a net gain.

The beauty of this perspective is that it flips failure on its head, which means that you're more willing to be courageous and try again. Your willingness to regather your resources, keep going and draw on your deep reserves of resilience will lead you to a life of greatness and fulfilment.

Despite the picture the media paints for us, the truth is that most people don't hit it out of the park on the first try, or even the second. The most remarkable writers, artists, investors, entrepreneurs, thinkers and scientists don't throw in the towel when their vested interests don't render a tangible result. They trust that it's not a loss – it's progress. It's tuition paid in exchange for insight, skill, wisdom, experience or knowledge.

So keep going. Stop letting sunk costs sink your self-worth. Pay your tuition with gratitude. Say thank you for the lessons. Then move on with the courage, creativity, confidence and pride of someone who is exceptionally well educated by this School of Life.

Go earn that PhD, boo. You got this.

THE VOID IS

NOT DEVOID

OF MEANING

& RICHNESS

THE VOID IS NOT DEVOID OF MEANING AND RICHNESS.

S ometimes we get confused and disconcerted by emptiness. We think it's a waiting room, a wasted space on our way somewhere else. We believe emptiness and quiet are somehow devoid of their own value and meaning. But here's the thing: the void is not devoid of meaning and richness. The void is an invitation into the energy of withdrawal, rest and emptying out. It's a valuable phase to be honoured and embraced.

So if you're feeling frustrated or uncertain or confused or overwhelmed by a space or emptiness in your life, that is perfect. Embrace it.

When you don't know what comes next, but you know you're done with the way things are – when you're in the void, sitting with the emptiness – ride that energy! Shed, shake, slip out of a skin, say 'no', say 'goodbye', scrub away, slough, scrap, separate, strike out and slash away what no longer serves.

Audit and edit your life – your space, closet, thoughts, habits, relationships and commitments – and identify what just ain't your jam anymore. Cut the shit. Carve out space. Consciously say 'no'. Start nothing new.

Dive into the fertile void: the emptiness and spaciousness of creative potential. Trust that what's coming is coming. Trust the presiding, orchestrating, universal cadence of life/death/life. For now, just kick it in the void.

Stop calling it a waiting room and start seeing it as a sacred space for rest and reflection. Surrender to the state of promise; sit with trust and the willingness to be surprised. It's all coming. It's all happening. New life is on its way. But first ... the fertile void. Don't wait impatiently. Be with it.

follow

THE

feels

FOLLOW THE FEELS.

We've learned to second-guess, to dumb down our intuition and instinct in favour of weighing careful columns of pros and cons. We overthink and under-feel. Look back at a decision you made in the past that just wasn't right (be it in business, life, relationships, anything). Think of something you took on that wasn't the right fit, or wasn't at the right time. Did you do your due diligence but still have a hunch that you ignored? Did some part of you feel it wasn't right? Did you trudge on anyway because of fear or logic? Did you think it was 'too good to miss', or that you 'might as well', or that there was 'no time like the present'?

How we make decisions is how our life unfolds. If we exclusively use logic and pie charts and pros and cons to make our decisions – and in doing so dismiss our gut feelings, intuition and instinct as unimportant, weak or witchy – we lose out. We walk uphill more than necessary. Our lives lack flow. We become prey. We become reactive. Decisions riddle us with anxiety. We vacillate, debate and nailbite. And then we often end up in situations that, well, suck – sometimes a little, and sometimes a lot.

Engaging our instincts isn't all rainbows and good vibes. It doesn't always give us the answers we want. But we must not throw away our gut feelings because they're hard, painful or intangible. Our instincts serve to protect and guide us, to shine light on our shadow sides and on external situations. Our instincts and intuition know what is best, what is good, what is right – and what is not.

If hindsight is 20/20, then intuitive foresight is 100/100.

You have instincts for a reason. Use them. Just follow the feels. The answer is there. You already know exactly what to do.

APPRECIATION

GO ON A

RAMPAGE

OF

APPRECIATION

GO ON A RAMPAGE OF APPRECIATION.

So often, we speed through our days with such velocity that we forget to slow down enough to say 'I see you. I love you. Thank you.'

When we do make time to spread some love, *it feels so good* – both for us and the receiver. We all know how even a small compliment or kindness makes us feel positively buoyant, sending us floating through the rest of our day.

Have you ever noticed how *you* feel lighter when you lift someone up? Appreciation is a win-win. So don't be lazy. Don't be stingy with your praise. Speak up. You have an unlimited, self-renewing bank account of love to draw from. In fact, the more you give, the more you have to give.

Sing your people's praises. Let them feel your love. Never underestimate the power you have to make someone's day. Dish out some good vibes today. Go on a rampage of appreciation.

DREAM SPECIFICALLY

DREAM SPECIFICALLY.

'Dream big' is something we hear a lot. But I think the size of our dreams is less important than the *specificity* of our dreams.

At first you might disagree with this statement, but take a beat and marinate on it. Consider one area of your life where you have a big goal or a big dream. Do you *really* know what you want? Could you fill an entire page with the details of that dream or goal? If I ask you, right now, to tell me what you want, *specifically*, I bet you couldn't.

We spend much of our lives working towards 'big' (actually vague) goals and dreams that we haven't even defined! It's no wonder we feel like we're chasing our tails sometimes. We can't achieve our dreams until we commit to them, and to commit to our dreams we need to know exactly what they are.

So stop dreaming big and start dreaming in specifics. Don't just draw a rough sketch of your dream – take the time to dream in full colour. How you define your dream is up to you. It might be expressed in qualities, images or even feelings. Write a story or a list. Fill a page. Sit with it. Erase and revise. Let it be a living document, free to be edited, full of life and rich in detail. The more precise and lifelike you make your dream, the more your dream can become your life.

So before you go chasing a dream, take the time to know what it is. Dream specifically.

YOUR SHADOW

IS NOTHING TO

BE ASHAMED OF

E very aspect of yourself that you judge or criticise or reject, every part of yourself that you blame or shame, becomes part of your shadow. Over time, your shadow embodies your shame. But listen up: your shadow is nothing to be ashamed of. It may seem dark and edgy, but it's mostly just misunderstood.

Your shadow began as a tiny thorn. Maybe that thorn came from a stem of self-judgement. Maybe that thorn was criticism misconstrued as fact. Maybe that thorn was a mistake made in innocence that was later infected with the anguish of regret and guilt. Maybe that thorn was the burden of someone else's unmet expectation. In silence and darkness, that speck of shame smouldered and grew hot, because that's the nature of shame: it festers in silence.

As the shame grew, so did your shadow – and, naturally, you wanted to distance yourself from it. So you disowned your shadow, afraid that it might overtake your light and snuff it out. You learned to live in fear of your darkness.

But here's the truth: your shadow doesn't conceal your light, it *complements* it. Just as nature is balanced by sun and moon, you've been gifted with light and shadow.

Think about it. We don't fear the night or worry that the sun won't shine in the morning; we embrace the qualities of each aspect. Each has a purpose. One is not better than the other – they're just different parts of a whole system.

The same is true of your light and your shadow. Both are worthy, and both are aspects of you that deserve your attention and respect.

It's time to unearth those parts of yourself that you misjudged and labelled 'unlovable'. It's time to dig out the parts of yourself that you have silenced and restrained and subdued in darkness. It's time to exhume the aspects of your you-ness that have been tainted with humiliation, comparison, regret, stigma or remorse. It's time to reclaim your shadow and re-examine it on your own terms.

Is there work to be done? Probably. But it's the shadow work that renders the richest returns. So don't be afraid of the dark. Rake through your shadow and see what treasure you can reclaim. >

When you rescue your shadow from the obscurity of shame and blame, you reap the harvest of your wholeness. Stop shaming your shadow and start dancing with it.

GO IT ALONE

GO IT ALONE.

Without solitude and quiet, we can never hear our inner guidance, our intuition or our instincts. Without inner guidance, we get stuck: stuck in the repetitions of the mind. Stuck outsourcing for information rather than tapping into our inner resources. Stuck navigating new territory with an old map. Stuck projecting old stories onto new experiences. Stuck in fear. Stuck cycling through the same bullshit that no longer serves us.

If you're feeling stuck in a cycle, go solo and get quiet. Go for a walk. Meditate. Take a long bath in silence. Write a letter to yourself. Make a cup of tea like it's a sacred ritual. Whatever way you can do it, go it alone and get quiet.

Give yourself high-quality alone time and you gift yourself access to the infinite goldmine of your intuitive resources. It's a sure-fire way to hit the reset button, crack open a can of fresh feels, unfold your map and trace your finger over a new route.

RIDE THE TIDES

RIDE THE TIDES.

The natural world offers us instruction in graceful transition. The sea doesn't strive; it doesn't worry when the tide goes out, fretting that the swell won't return. And when it feels its energy mounting, the sea doesn't stifle the swell, worrying that its weight rushing onto the shore is too much, too fast, too vast. The sea honours the ebb and flow.

The natural world gives itself over to the pulsing cadence of life. Nature freezes and becomes still, quakes and quivers, bursts forth into bloom, goes to seed. Nature vibrates, ripples, swells, recedes and surges. Nature feasts and nature fasts. Nature produces and nature rests. The cycles complete themselves, creating an overall evenness, wholeness and integration.

As human beings, our involuntary, innate rhythms are the same. Our lives are seasonal. Our breaths are tidal. Our bodies are cyclical. Our emotions are fluid. Our creativity and energy and appetites wax and wane. Everything changes and then changes again, just as it should.

We are living, pulsating creatures. Each of us is an integrated whole, an effortlessly organised sum of parts. Fluid, ever-changing, moving, thrusting and receding, but *whole*. Rhythmic. Unified.

It is safe to trust in the tides of your life. Your trust creates graceful transition. Embrace the wisdom of your wild nature and tune in to your innate ability to embrace the changing tides of energy, abundance, creativity and inner resources.

Ride the tide of your humanness. Release your grip and step into the flow. Trust the timing and tides of your life. Cultivate grace as you ebb and flow, in trust.

CLARITY and COURAGE ARE THE CIRCUITRY of INNER TRUST

CLARITY AND COURAGE ARE THE CIRCUITRY OF INNER TRUST.

The more you trust yourself, the better decisions you make; the better decisions you make, the more you trust yourself. This is the vital rhythm of an inner life built on clarity and courage.

But how do you develop and deepen your trust in yourself? How do you calibrate yourself to clarity and uncage your courage?

The same way you build trust in all of your relationships: by being in dialogue, by striking the balance of receptivity and responsiveness. First, attuning to attentive listening. Then, honouring the information offered by taking conscious action. This process creates a cycle of intuition and action that builds the circuitry of inner trust.

Having a hard time hearing yourself? Riddled with self-doubt? Try these three steps:

* **Meditate on the regular:** Meditation dials down the outer noise, sweeps away the mental static and makes it easier to perceive trustworthy inner messages with clarity.

* **Pay exquisite attention:** Guidance comes in many forms. Pay attention to the ideas that spring forth suddenly and unexpectedly, the feelings that set your heart alight, the instinctual, animal impulses. These are all messengers.

* **Take aligned action:** When you are pinged with guidance, *act!* Do not ignore it. Take action aligned with the information you've received. Watch what happens. Acting on the wise counsel your inner guidance offers creates positive outcomes in your life. The more you do it, the more it builds confidence and courage, thereby stamping out the self-doubt that clogs the circuitry of your inner guidance and self-trust.

Clarity and courage are the circuitry of inner trust. So intuit, then act. Watch how your life unfolds differently when you trust yourself.

YOU DON'T HAVE TIME TO RUSH

YOU DON'T HAVE TIME TO RUSH.

O verwhelmed? In a rush? Don't have time? But first ... coffee/inbox/ start the laundry? Scratch that. Here's the truth: life happens fast. You don't have time to rush.

Remind yourself how precious your attention is, how fleeting the moments of your life are. Some moments feel like an eternity, a trial of patience. But overall, the years pass at lightning speed. Blink (or be distracted) and you'll miss it.

You can't press pause on joy or fast-forward through challenges. All you can do is be present and pay attention as life unfolds, soaking up each detail of each moment with every cell in your body.

Slow down enough to be with each breath, each frame, each note. Saturate yourself in presence. Record every moment in your heart. Life happens fast. You don't have time to rush.

MOBILISE GRATITUDE AND GRATITUDE MOBILISES YOU

MOBILISE GRATITUDE AND GRATITUDE MOBILISES YOU.

I f you don't know where you're going, if you're feeling defeated, overwhelmed or stuck in a cycle of negativity, if your future feels postponed in perpetuity, take stock of how far you've come. Use the positivity of the past to improve the present.

Trace your finger over the trail of your past years – the map of your life so far: the terrain you've travelled, the rivers you've crossed. Look at all the ground you've covered.

Stocktake your blessings, your progress, your points of pride and the pieces of your life that did, in fact, go according to plan. Even the mistakes – and the disguised gifts they offered – are worthy of your gratitude.

Count them out. Turn them over in your palms. Let them reflect back to you all that is good, all that is great, all that is better than it was before.

Pay attention to your progress. Attune yourself to gratitude. Let it soothe the inner strife, the stuckness, the uncertainty, the fear and the doubt.

Remind yourself that there is still so much to be grateful for, and that there is more goodness coming.

Mobilise gratitude and gratitude mobilises you.

BREAKDOWN TO

BREAKTHROUGH

The step-by-step process to evolve:

* Breakdown

* Breakthrough.

Transformation is not a lukewarm, part-time hobby you dabble in. Your growth, your personal evolution, is a process of creative destruction, not a casual pastime.

No matter how many self-help books you read or weekend workshops you attend, no matter how many times you go to yoga in a week, the truth is: you have to be willing to evolve.

Being willing to evolve means that you are willing to sacrifice yourself at the altar of transformation. You must be willing to do the hard work of telling your truth; willing to see things differently; willing to be consumed by the process; willing to be devoured by the fires of transformation; willing to be a hot mess, at least for a minute. You must be willing to be temporarily dismantled, to feel lost, to break *down*. You must be willing to sacrifice the way you are for who you can become, for the person you will be.

Your need to evolve presses itself against the boundaries you've constructed around who you think you are. It's uncomfortable at best, and often painfully confronting. But there is beauty in the breakdown. You'll only break through when you've surrendered to the process; when you've scrubbed yourself red and raw, clean of half-truths; when you've given shame the cold shoulder and told the truth about how you feel, what you're afraid of and what you want.

Remember this: your need for transformation is the transformative aspect itself. It's a call from the very seat of your soul that rings through your cells, beckoning you to *become* – to become more of who you are.

Just like the birth of stars, the evolution of our selves happens under pressure and then explodes exquisitely across the landscape of our lives.

Breakdown. Breakthrough.

The beauty is on the other side.

THERE

IS

magic

IN THE

MUNDANE

THERE IS MAGIC IN THE MUNDANE.

I t can feel like the mundane dominates our days with necessities and duties. We must be careful not to let the rhythmic trance of the mundane blind us to moments of beauty and bliss (no matter how fleeting they may be).

In between the piles of laundry and list-making and emailing and endless tidying up and nappy-changing and meal planning and refereeing and coaxing and all the other things that can make the days feel like an endless string of reruns, there is always a little bit of bliss, a little bit of beauty, a dash of the divine, a morsel of majesty or mystery. There are sweet, magical moments wedged in between the mundane.

The mundane is the engine that keeps the wheels rolling, but the magic is what fuels the tank.

So remember to make space for magic amid the mundane machinations of your day. Pause. Notice. Linger a little longer. Take a deeper breath. Open your eyes a little wider. Pay attention to the way sunlight streams in through the kitchen window, warming whatever it touches. Let yourself receive the loveliness of a smile from someone's lips. Awaken to the unseen miracle of your breath; to the artistry of flowers and stars and moonlight; to the bliss of a balmy breeze on bare skin; to the smell of fresh laundry, dried beneath a blue sky; to the taste of honey on toast.

The truth is, your day is full of tiny wonders and itty-bitty delicacies. There is always magic amid the mundane and beauty in the banal. So let your day be a treasure hunt. Capture each delight with every single sense. Tuck them into the folds of your heart. Let these shimmering morsels of mystery and majesty and miraculousness fuel you as you roll on through the routine.

BE MORE OF _____YOU_____.

BE MORE OF YOU.

B ecoming your best self is not a process of addition, but subtraction. It's a process of stripping off the layers of fear, shame and unworthiness that drive reactivity, negativity, anxiety and self-doubt.

It's not a process of fixing and adding; it's a process of freeing and deducting, of liberating yourself from the bullshit that has been built around you. It's seeing the untruths of your unworthiness, the misconceptions and messages you've received, and shaking them off to reveal your true nature.

You are already whole, worthy, wise and wonderful. You don't need to become someone new.

You don't have to fix yourself up to become your best self. Courage, patience, compassion and grace are your natural states. It's all there, always, waiting to be uncovered. And when it is, we all get the best of you – and that creates a positive ripple effect that touches every edge of your life.

So when you think about making resolutions or kicking off a new habit, remember: this is not self-improvement, it's self-revelation. It's about revealing your divine nature – and remembering that you are a drop in the ocean divine. It's about living with intention and purpose and courage, so you can share your gifts fully.

The point of all this is not to become someone new, it's to be *more* of you.

PAY

ATTENTION

TO

YOUR

PROGRESS

PAY ATTENTION TO YOUR PROGRESS.

If you are heavy with uncertainty; if you're feeling stunted, short-changed, stuck, isolated or overwhelmed; if freedom and possibility feel in short supply; if plans are postponed, futures are uncertain or efforts for forward momentum are frozen in their tracks; if you feel like you're spinning your wheels or sliding backwards – please, don't let the little victories and forward footsteps fall through the cracks of your attention. Stop looking at the big picture. Shrink your attention. Refine your focus. Start thinking *small*.

Make this your mantra: pay attention to your progress – however small, however slow, however humble. Name all the ways you are making progress, even in the midst of challenge.

Not all is lost, so please don't stop. Keep going. Keep being brave with your life. Stop waiting for the finish line. Let go of the timelines. Let yourself be in the process. Then pay attention to your progress.

LET YOURSELF HAVE THE MOMENT.

LET YOURSELF HAVE THE MOMENT.

LET YOURSELF HAVE THE MOMENT.

LET YOURSELF HAVE THE MOMENT.

LET YOURSELF HAVE THE MOMENT.

LET YOURSELF HAVE THE MOMENT.

LET YOURSELF HAVE THE MOMENT.

LET YOURSELF HAVE THE MOMENT.

LET YOURSELF HAVE THE MOMENT.

LET YOURSELF HAVE THE MOMENT.

LET YOURSELF HAVE THE MOMENT.

LET YOURSELF HAVE THE MOMENT.

LET YOURSELF HAVE THE MOMENT.

LET YOURSELF HAVE THE MOMENT.

LET YOURSELF HAVE THE MOMENT.

LET YOURSELF HAVE THE MOMENT.

LET YOURSELF HAVE THE MOMENT.

We are so busy being busy, so rushed from all the rushing around, spread so thin from so much simultaneous doing. The (often overlooked, but very meaningful) consequence of all that busyness and multitasking and rushing is that we are accidentally denying ourselves the most nourishing aspect of life: presence.

A habitual lack of presence can make life feel wildly exhausting, impossibly overwhelming and deeply unsatisfying. Why? Because presence is the portal through which we access joy, peace, pleasure, connection and satisfaction. By never letting ourselves be fully present, we are suffocating the most meaningful and pleasurable aspects of life.

Next time you're tempted to overlap two (or more!) activities in the name of productivity, take a breath and wiggle your toes. Land in the moment. There is room to breathe and pleasure to receive. It's yours. Give yourself over to it. Let yourself have it.

The kiss. The hot cup of coffee. The square of chocolate. The slow morning. The game of Scrabble.

The walk. The song. The weekend paper. The lunchbreak. The phone call. The drive. The pedicure.

The boiling of water for tea. The slicing of vegetables. The moment.

Be here with it.

GIVE

YOUR GIFTS

FORGET THE

REST

GIVE YOUR GIFTS, FORGET THE REST.

C omparing is competing. Competing is striving. Striving is ego. Ego is pain. Pain blocks joy. So when you're cruising along, feeling pretty good, and you slip into a pothole of comparison, remember this: you are on your personal path, your own journey. Trust in its unfolding. Your personal story and your unique experience form the fabric of your authenticity. Your authenticity is the key to unlock all the opportunities, gifts and joy in life that are meant for you.

Being authentically you and trusting in your unique path is the only way to access and experience your true, full potential. Otherwise, you're just chasing down everyone else's dharma and foolishly overlooking your own.

Revere the truth and timing of your life. Don't compare their apples with your oranges. Bypass comparison, that crazy bish. Just do you. Follow your path. Give your gifts. Trust. Forget the rest.

BE
AVAILABLE
TO BE
INSPIRED

BE AVAILABLE TO BE INSPIRED.

I f you want to up your creative game, you need to be *available* to be inspired. Here's what I mean: inspiration can't find you if you're sitting in a cramped cubicle for twelve hours a day, or watching some shitty prime-time soap opera, or gossiping, or stifling your feelings, or pushing yourself harder to be perfect.

Inspiration finds you with your hair tousled, your back pressed to the earth and your eyes gazing across the open sky. Inspiration finds you in truthful, candlelit conversation with wild-hearted kindreds. Inspiration finds you at the bottom of a teacup and in the last sentence of a good book. Inspiration finds you in the throes of deeply feeling what you're feeling. Inspiration finds you with your feet bare and your face turned to the sun. Inspiration finds you when you're truly absorbed in the moments of your life. Inspiration finds you holding a pen or paintbrush to paper. Inspiration finds you in a state of surrender, lying flat on your belly, palms upturned. Inspiration finds you when you move your body joyfully – sweetly and gently, or vigorously and wildly. Inspiration finds you when you get still and quiet – when you listen.

Inspiration is waiting to rise up, to flow through you, to dash down from the heavens and spark a thought thunderbolt. You just have to be there to receive it.

Create the conditions for creativity to flow through you. You already know, intuitively, what the conditions are for you. So make space and let it happen. Invite inspiration into your life. Be available to be inspired.

REALISE THAT
YOU ARE
already
complete
& YOU BECOME
FULLY
REALISED

YOU'RE ALREADY COMPLETE AND YOU BECOME FULLY REALISED.

If you struggle with feeling incomplete or lost or not enough, fret not. You have everything you need. You aren't broken or missing any pieces. Perhaps it's just that you haven't fully awakened to your full, in-born potential. Perhaps you've been pushed down, stifled or suffocated. Perhaps you have been shaped and moulded into something other than your youest you.

Every time you were told to be quieter or louder, more demure or more brave, to be smarter or to downplay your wits, to be not so serious or more serious, thinner or heavier: another layer. Every time you were told you weren't pretty enough, or made to feel ashamed of your beauty: another layer. Every time you were told to tone it down, to be less brazen or bold, or to speak up and stop being so meek: another layer. Every time someone shushed a raucous round of laughter, or told you not to sing, or said your personality was too big, or scolded you for being inappropri-ate, or told you that outfit wasn't for you, or laughed at your question, or raised an eyebrow at your dance moves, or told you to get your head out of the clouds: another layer. Every perceived failure, every moment of shame: another layer.

And so you learn to value the propaganda of others' beliefs and opinions (which are almost always rooted in their own fears, insecuri-ties, shame and 'I-am-not-enough' stories) above the untainted infor-mation of your own inklings, instincts, intuition, proclivities and blissful leanings (which are the shape of your soul).

The shape of your soul, it's there – unchanging, waiting to be un-earthed and discovered. It's waiting for you to chip away at the false walls, the cheap cladding, the layers of protection that have been caked on over the years to form a facade that takes the shape of who you think you're supposed to be, and betrays the shape of who you really are.

Don't fret that you're incomplete. Don't seek outside of yourself. It's all already there. Your only work is to unearth yourself from the lay-ers of bullshit you've been dutifully building up as evidence in the case of your not-enoughness. Take an axe to it. Tear it down.   ❯

You will work softly and gently at first, timid and unsure. But then, as you scrape back the layers, you'll pick up the scent. Your work will become fervorous, joyful and focused, yet free – like a horse galloping home through a familiar, open field.

Realise that you are already complete and you become fully realised. It's that hard. It's that easy.

PRESENCE

IS THE
CURRENCY
OF

CONNECTION

L earning to be present with your whole self – rather than being lost in thought or rehearsing what you'll say next – is the greatest gift you can give those you love. Your family, friends and co-workers will feel heard and seen, which translates into more intimacy and trust with those who matter most. Presence really is the currency of connection.

Here's a cheat sheet for deepening presence in six simple steps:

* **Let yourself land:** Wiggle your toes, take a breath into your belly and land in the moment. It can help to tune in to sensations in your body or the scents and sounds in the space around you.

* **Make it friendly:** Think of the moment itself as a companion. Meet it as a friend that is full of life, not as a void that needs to be filled.

* **Be receptive:** Lay down the doing. Set aside the striving. Invite in a sense of receptivity: a willingness to receive the moment as it is, to receive others just as they are.

* **Listen well:** When others are speaking, try to listen without attending to your wants or fears and without preparing a response. Notice the ways you might want to direct, control or prove. Then choose to soften.

* **Bring curiosity:** Leaning in to curiosity (rather than judgement, criticism or preconceived opinions) helps us open up to every experience, and to each other, with more compassion and courage. When it's your turn to speak, explore whether you can compose questions instead of statements. 'I wonder', 'What if' and 'How would it feel' are all great openers.

* **Come back:** If you leave, notice, take a breath and return (over and over again). Like meditation, presence is a practice.

Bottom line: presence really is the greatest gift we can offer each other. Try out these six steps and explore how deepening your presence with others can result in more satisfying relationships across the board. I think you'll find that presence is a gift that gives back.

This formula not only applies to how you relate to others, but also to how you relate to yourself. Our ability to connect and find intimacy with others is in direct proportion to our ability to do so with ourselves.

IMPERFECT MOMENTS MATTER
IMPERFECT MOMENTS MATTER
IMPERFECT MOMENTS MATTER
IMPERFECT MOMENTS MATTER
IMPERFECT MOMENTS MATTER
IMPERFECT MOMENTS MATTER
IMPERFECT MOMENTS MATTER
IMPERFECT MOMENTS MATTER

IMPERFECT MOMENTS MATTER.

May we remember that while the beautiful moments take our breath away and look good on paper, the less-than-perfect moments connect us through the rawness of reality.

May we remember that the pursuit of perfection is more painful and less fruitful than it's worth, and that life's pleasures are more often found in the imperfect moments. The imperfect moments are often those punctuated with laughter, and laughter shakes us out of the trance of seriousness and striving. May we remember to lighten up and have fun. May we remember to laugh at ourselves.

May we remember to never compare our behind-the-scenes life to someone else's highlight reel. And may we remember to *include* imperfect moments in our highlight reel.

Afraid of being judged? Don't be. People won't love you less for keeping it real, baring your wounds or broadcasting your bloopers. Quite the opposite: they'll relate and connect to you more deeply. They'll honour you for the bravery behind your honesty. They'll laugh with you. They'll cry with you. They'll love you thoroughly.

Include imperfections and they become possibilities for deeper connection. Imperfect moments matter.

FREEDOM
IS ON THE OTHER SIDE
OF CHOICE

FREEDOM IS ON THE OTHER SIDE OF CHOICE.

Sometimes it's hard to say yes. Sometimes it's hard to say no. Sometimes the hardest thing is to begin something, and sometimes the hardest thing is to finish it. Sometimes the only thing to do next is to just keep going. And sometimes the only thing to do next is to let it go.

Choices can come coupled with uncertainty. Sometimes you sit in the dark, wondering what to do next. Sometimes you weep at providence's feet, begging for a set of ordained instructions or a map to your destiny.

Sometimes the sign you're waiting for isn't coming. Sometimes the heavens won't deliver a solution or an answer or a miracle. Sometimes you just have to make a decision, have a hard conversation or take a leap of faith.

Choice is difficult by design, because it's a crossroads: an intersection of options that can escalate into a crisis of uncertainty.

Confronting the choice demands that you address the thing you've been avoiding. It stops the music on the dance of evasion and challenges you to square off with what you've been postponing, pushing down or sidestepping.

Sometimes the choice comes down to how badly you want something. Sometimes it's a question of how deeply you don't. Sometimes it's a question of how much you believe. Sometimes it's a question of how sincerely you crave freedom.

Sometimes it's a question posed between equally valid options. Sometimes it's a question that's not a question but a pretence – one option masquerading as two. Sometimes it's a question of whether you're going to be soft and gentle and good to yourself by being firm and fierce with others. Sometimes it's a question of what you think you're worth.

Whatever the nature of the choice, procrastination is futile. If you avoid the choice, it will hang around, patiently waiting for an opportunity to insert itself into the curriculum of your growth.

When you finally face it, when you're called to commit to an answer, your confidence might evaporate. You might feel adrift. Your voice might shake and your bones might rattle in response. Your hand might hesitate as you draw a boundary or sign on the dotted line. >

You might play a few raucous rounds of second-guessing. But all of this hesitation, wavering, alternating and waffling is unnecessary.

Because whatever the choice, these things are true: you already know the right choice for you, and freedom is on the other side.

So don't be held hostage by hesitation. Choose – no matter how robust the resistance seems – because the nature of progress is moving through resistance. Then liberate yourself by committing to the choice and wherever it takes you next.

Challenging choices are presented not to bury you, but to elevate you – to strengthen your resolve, to clarify your aim and to refine your fluency in the language of your instincts. Committing to your choice is a doorway into the future. A choice is a call to dive through the resistance, commit to what's next and rise up to meet it. So make that damn choice. You got this. Freedom is on the other side.

TAKE

RESPONSIBILITY

FOR YOUR

EXPERIENCE

TAKE RESPONSIBILITY FOR YOUR EXPERIENCE.

Sometimes shit happens. Sometimes things don't go to plan. People are late. Targets are missed. Cars break. Planes are delayed. Baggage is lost. Friends let us down. Investments crash. It's inevitable that we are going to meet these kinds of experiences over the course of our lives.

While you won't always be in control of your circumstances (*what* you're experiencing) you are always responsible for *how* you experience your circumstances.

When we spend our days blaming people or circumstances for our funky vibes and bad moods, we're giving away our power. When we take back responsibility for our inner landscape we are free to choose.

In other words, bad things might happen, but you don't have to feel bad about it. Shitty, sad, frustrating things might happen, but, more often than not, you can choose to rise above it. Shrug it off. Smile your way through it. Laugh if you can. Take it with a grain of salt. Zoom out. Take a breath.

Your mood, your vibe and the flavour of your experience are determined by the one and only *you*. Take back ownership of your experience and you'll realise that your experience is entirely up to you.

SOMETIMES, THE ONLY THING TO DO IS NOTHING

SOMETIMES, THE ONLY THING TO DO IS NOTHING.

G ive yourself permission to be goalless. Set aside the need to achieve. Put your feet up and your to-do list down. Give all those 'shoulds' the cold shoulder.

Let your goals wait – they'll still be standing to attention when you return. Take a mental holiday, however momentary.

Untie yourself from the shores of determination and set yourself adrift. Just float, belly turned skyward, arms spread wide. Feel your buoyancy. Do nothing.

For fifteen minutes, or an afternoon, or a day: revel in rest. Regroup. Restore yourself. Regather your resources.

Because sometimes, the only thing to do is nothing.

USE YOUR IMAGINATION WISELY

USE YOUR IMAGINATION WISELY

USE YOUR IMAGINATION WISELY

USE YOUR IMAGINATION WISELY

USE YOUR IMAGINATION WISELY.

I f you're telling yourself a story, it's easy to let it burn like wildfire and swallow up the entire landscape of your life. Be mindful of the way you engage with the stories you tell yourself – whether they're stories of busyness, overwhelm, self-doubt or stuckness. Be especially conscious of those you label 'challenges'.

In small ways, we feed ourselves a regular diet of information that grows the feelings and outcomes we *don't* want. Not only is this a self-perpetuating cycle of negativity, but it has larger implications. What we speak about, what we think about and what we imagine are what we create in life. Focus on the lack in your life and you'll get more lack. Focus on how much chocolate you're eating and all you'll think about is eating more chocolate. Focus on your spending and you'll spend more. Any of that ring a bell?

Watch what you (and those around you) think and say. 'I'm so busy.' 'I'm totally overwhelmed.' 'Money is tight.' 'I'm tired.' 'Things are really hard right now.' 'I don't have enough time.' 'I'm really lonely.' That's not language that invites in new possibilities; it's language that keeps you stuck. It is what author Wayne Dyer often called 'a misuse of imagination'.

So do a little system upgrade to make sure you're using your imagination wisely. Spark a story of flow, fulfilment and abundance and let it spread through your imagination like a sunrise.

Here are three ways to spark a new story:

* **Flip the script:** Every time you notice a negative thought (a thought about what you *don't* want to happen), flip the script and turn it into a positive statement that illustrates the feelings and outcomes you *do* want.

* **Upgrade your words:** Whenever you're about to say something about lack or doubt, upgrade it. Replace it with something that affirms what you desire, not what you fear. >

* **Check your inputs:** Notice whether you are feeding yourself an unhelpful diet of negativity. Maybe it's a profile on Instagram that generates 'I'm not enough' feels for you. Maybe it's overdosing on a certain kind of podcast or book. Maybe it's the TV shows you're bingeing. Maybe it's the people you're surrounding yourself with, or the conversations you're having with them. Check your inputs and unsubscribe from the shit that feeds negative patterns.

Use your imagination wisely and go spark a new story, sweet thing!

IF THEY BURN YOU OUT, CUT 'EM OUT. IF THEY LIGHT YOU UP, FEED THE FLAME.

IF THEY BURN YOU OUT, CUT 'EM OUT.
IF THEY LIGHT YOU UP, FEED THE FLAME.

M otivational speaker Jim Rohn famously said, 'You are the average of the five people you spend the most time with.' *Believe* that, y'all!

We can talk about it in terms of sums and averages, but here's another way to say it: life is all about resonance. It's our nature as human beings to resonate with what surrounds us. We want to relate, we want to connect and we want to make others feel comfortable. So if you're hanging with people who are doing low-vibe things, you're going to vibrate on that level *with* them. And if you surround yourself with people who are vibrating higher, you're going to rise up and meet them there.

So be conscious of who you surround yourself with. Notice how you feel around them. Do you feel inspired? Deeply connected? Uplifted? Like you can be yourself? Like you are loved? If the answer is yes, feed those relationships. If the answer is no, drop 'em like it's hot, 'cause it's time for an upgrade.

In short: if they burn you out, cut 'em out. If they light you up, feed the flame.

HOW YOU DO ANYTHING

IS

HOW YOU DO EVERYTHING

HOW YOU DO ANYTHING IS HOW YOU DO EVERYTHING.

P aying bills, cooking dinner, changing nappies, taking phone calls, returning emails, exercising, making tea, folding laundry, filing paperwork ... These can all feel like a series of boxes to tick, an endless chain of the mundane.

But remember: you get to choose whether you trudge through tasks or whether you do them with joy, devotion, presence, gratitude and pleasure. No matter how mundane, mindless, repetitive or meaningless these tasks may seem, they are an opportunity to train yourself in the art of presence and intention. With the power of your attention and your intention, you can make the repetitious into a ritual, the mundane into the magical.

So choose to make your life a moving meditation. With every task, every effort, every conversation, every moment, remind yourself: 'How I do this is how I do everything.'

YOUR INTENTION BECOMES YOUR INHERITANCE

BECOMES YOUR INHERITANCE YOUR INTENTION

YOUR INTENTION BECOMES YOUR INHERITANCE.

W ho you are is a changing proposition. Don't feel stuck. If there's some way you've been pigeonholed or even cajoled into a role that isn't really yours, shake it off. Mix it up.

Who you are is entirely up to you. This life is yours. If you want to write yourself into a new story, you are free to do so. Pull up a fresh page. Update your bio. Forecast some future feels for yourself! What you dream up for yourself *now* becomes your reality *next*.

So what will it be? If you're not sure where to start, if intention setting makes you feel frozen with indecision, try this: spend ten minutes writing a bio for future you. Maybe it's five or ten years from now, or thirty or forty.

Here are some questions to consider as you write your bio that can light the way for your future self: What do you value? What matters? Who matters most to you and who do you matter to most? What makes your cells sing? What makes you come alive? What do you stand for? What do you offer the world? How are you generous? What do you share? What is rewarding for you? What does living a brave life look like? How do you feel? How do you make others feel?

Take some time to think about the dreams you can bestow upon your future self. Because your intention becomes your inheritance.

claim your
power

own your
worth

CLAIM YOUR POWER, OWN YOUR WORTH.

Many of us have lost our ability to discern who's worthy of determining our worth. We've set up a system whereby we seek to reclaim our power over and over again. How? People pleasing, overusing the word 'yes', obsessively consulting our social media accounts, tallying up likes and comments, taking jobs we don't want, dating people we don't love and earning degrees we don't need, and then measuring ourselves against others and getting snagged in the wily trap of comparison.

We're praise junkies, looking for any opportunity to get another hit – to stand out, to be admired, to feel special, to get the grade. We're auctioneers, letting bystanders' bids determine our worth. We're beggars, appealing to others in the hope we might hear the clinging of their coins of esteem, thanks or approval dropping into our cup.

If you are stuck in this cycle of perpetually proving yourself, you're letting others hold your power. If you let others judge your worthiness, you also give them authority over your sense of wholeness.

The only way to liberate yourself from the fruitless grind of auctioneering, racking up stats and begging for praise is to reclaim your power and evaluate your own self-worth. This takes a robust inner guidance system, but that can be developed – through stillness.

The prerequisites are a willingness to listen and the confidence to act on what you hear. You must tune your ear to the song of your intuition and wrap your actions in trust.

With time, you'll develop your own standards. You'll become more and more autonomous. Taking back your power calls you to the frontier, where there are no external signposts or distance markers – just you and the wilderness of your inner world. You'll throw the reins loose and listen to the instincts that are your birthright, guiding you back to the inherent wholeness and worthiness that are already within you.

That goodness is yours. Take it. Because when you claim your power, you own your worth.

CHALLENGES ARE
AN INVITATION FROM
THE DIVINE

CHALLENGES ARE AN INVITATION FROM THE DIVINE.

When it feels like an uphill battle, like things will never change or it's all too hard, remember this: challenges are an invitation from the divine into another layer of expansion, into a greater capacity for life.

This path you're on, this work you're confronted with, this pain you're looking in the eye, this challenge that's looming – it's a clarion call, beckoning you to grow, progress and move forwards. It's a summons from the divine, urging you to do the work, unravel the knots and smooth out the creases, rewrite an old story, make a different choice, stretch yourself and continue on the path of your own becoming.

Does nature leave budding flowers to wither away, suspended in an unrealised state, and say 'Good enough, that'll do'? Does winter linger in perpetuity? Does the moon yawn at the sea and think, 'Maybe tomorrow'?

No. Just as nature expects the ecstatic bloom to burst forth from the bud, just as spring leaps forward from the depths of winter, just as the moon sings up the tides, so does the divine call out to you, summoning your greatness, your growth and your full potential.

This is the pulse and the power and the momentum of love that flows from the divine to you. So reframe your labouring, your suffering and your challenges as summons from the divine: as loving invitations, asking nothing of you other than that you become fully yourself.

this day is a gift.

AND SO ARE YOU.

THIS DAY IS A GIFT. AND SO ARE YOU.

Whatever happened yesterday, no matter how you slipped or faltered, regardless of the ways you betrayed your best or covered over your inborn excellence – today is new.

Just like that, you get another shot. Another day to be grateful for. Another glimpse at your potential. Another chance at compassion, kindness, presence and joy. The boon of a new beginning.

So be willing to begin again, to be reborn as your best self. Take the chance at a new day. Take it in your arms, bundle it up and keep it close to your heart. Run with it. Give it all the love and gratitude and greatness that you have.

This day is a gift. And so are you. Now, go, you good thing. Start anew. Start now. Go give your gifts today.

SIMPLY BY

BEING

MADE, YOU

WERE

MADE TO

BELONG

I f you have spent your life earning your worth, bartering for belonging, scraping together a sense of wholeness, hustling up security paid for in tit-for-tat instalments, let me ask you: who decided you didn't belong? Who decided you weren't enough? Who said you weren't already intrinsically worthy and whole, and a part of not just something but everything? Who told you this lie for the very first time?

Because, dear one, this idea that you weren't already perfectly formed and made for this world is not just improbable but impossible.

Your belonging is not something to be weighed and measured or calculated and earned. Your belonging is not evaluated by application once you have become something more. Your belonging began the very moment the first cells of your being started to quiver and shake. That was your invitation and your initiation.

Who looks at the mountain and says: 'Just a bit out of place'?

Who says to the river: 'A little more to the right'?

Who tells the sun: 'Turn it down a notch'?

Who orders the moon: 'Stop changing shape'?

Who tsks at the tussock grasses for dancing in the wind?

Who raises an eyebrow at how quietly the tree breathes?

Who whispers to the lake: 'I wish you were an ocean'?

Who tells the cloud: 'You aren't meant to be here'?

Who scolds the lichen: 'Don't cling so tightly'?

Who tells the flower: 'You're a petal short'?

No one. Not you, not me, not God or the divine or nature itself. And if all of that, all of creation, is good enough, just as it's made, why wouldn't you be, too?

What if, from this day forwards, you gazed upon yourself like a mountain, a lake, the sun, the moon, a tree or a tussock blade bowing in the wind? What if you remembered that you, too, are a creation of the divine natural world? You are a creation that does not need to be critiqued, judged, fixed or altered; a creation that does not need to earn its place in the world; a creation that is welcomed, accepted, embraced and beloved for all of the qualities it brings to life. >

Simply by being made, you were made to belong. Belonging is in your bones and your blood. Belonging is your birthright, your inheritance from the divine: forever flowing to you and through you. You belong.

So, please, show us your softness and your rocky edges; show us the ways you shine and blossom and how you dance in the wind. Show us your depths, your heights. Show us your uneven petals and the ways you are quiet. Show us the storms and let us also stand in your sunshine. Show us the many shapes you take. Show us all of you.

Because like everything in nature, you are divine, and you fit perfectly into this world. Simply by being, you belong.

don't settle
into the
setback

DON'T SETTLE INTO THE SETBACK.

I grew up riding horses on our family ranch. The thing I most remember my parents saying to me after I'd fallen or been bucked off is 'Get back on the horse'. Right then and there. And I always did.

If you didn't get back in the saddle, the price you'd pay was a persistent fear that would settle into your bones (not to mention a horse that thought it could get away with it again). So I'd dust myself off and climb back in the saddle. This was training in the practice of resilience: making a habit of rising up from the cloud of dust and going again.

If you've been bucked by life lately, if you're feeling like you've failed, if you're feeling timid, if you're doing that diabolical dance of one step forwards and two steps back, I feel you. Take a moment. Take a breath. Take it for what it is. Re-evaluate. Reset. Reboot. Change tack. Ask for help. Think it through. And then get back on your horse.

I'm not saying you should keep going at all costs, or push yourself just to push yourself. I'm saying don't settle into the setback when the stakes are high, when it matters, when you know you can do better. Take a hot minute to gather your wits and then get back in the saddle. There's something wonderful coming – a breakthrough, a new vista, a fresh experience – so giddy up and ride on. Show that (metaphorical) horse (and yourself) who's boss.

f*ck the hustle. follow the flow.

D on't tell Jay-Z, but it turns out you *can* knock the hustle. Let me be clear: I'm all for a strong work ethic, passion and motivation. I'm all about big dreams and kicking goals. But I'm not down with the cultural glorification of the hustle. It's so 1996. Flow is the new hustle.

Here's how I see it: hustling is forceful. It's pushing and aggressively 'chasing' our dreams, at all costs. And sometimes those costs are high – exhaustion, depletion, frayed relationships and missed signs, to name a few.

When we hustle, we're so focused on our goal that we lose sight of the big picture. Our heads are down; we're charging forwards with blinders on. We miss the signs that sometimes come our way, suggesting we reroute or change course. We're so focused on the outcome that we forget the importance of the process and the value of being willing to head in a different direction.

Hustling asks us to override the seasonal, cyclical aspect of our energy, creativity and inspiration. It demands that we be in a perpetual summer, when sometimes we desperately need to sink into the hibernation of winter to restore ourselves and regather our resources (creative and otherwise). Sure, we can get results in the short-term, but by refusing to honour our cycles in the long-term we head straight towards burnout.

The reality is we're too afraid to rest – because beneath the pride of hustling is the fear of failure. Operating from a place of fear is never a good strategy long-term. Feeling fear is super useful when you're being chased by a bear; not so useful when you're building a business, pursuing a passion or working on your wellness. When we're in a place of fear, we can't possibly align ourselves with the energy we need to manifest anything positive.

So in this world where we've been taught to hustle and drive for results, what do we do instead? Focus on stepping into the flow. Slow your roll. Honour your creative and energetic cycles. Stay true to your passion. Mind your intuition. Pay attention to the signs. Change your course accordingly. You're being guided, so act like it. Remember that the process is usually just as valuable as the outcome and that a holistic, flexible progression can actually deliver richer results.

In other words, don't chase your dreams; instead, let them lead you. F*ck the hustle. Follow the flow.

WHAT IF YOU
believed
YOU
WERE
ALREADY
enough?

WHAT IF YOU BELIEVED YOU WERE ALREADY ENOUGH?

H ow would that change the way you feel about your day? The things you need to do? The things you should or shouldn't have said?

What could you do with your time, energy and focus if you weren't out there hustling up another hit of self-worth with endless people pleasing and empty overachieving?

If you believed you were already enough, what would you have the courage to do today? Who would you say no to? What would you say yes to? What would you ask for? What would you speak up about? How would you start your day? How would you end it? And with whom?

Now, tally up your answers. How does all that sound? Like a big f*ck-ing relief? Like a dream day? I have great news: you *are* already enough. Right now. You're good. You're great! You don't need to go and earn your worth today, love. You just need to act like you're already worth it – because you are.

Let that truth shape your day.

SURRENDER IS WHAT LETS YOU DANCE WITH THE DIVINE

S urrender. Does that word trigger you a bit? Me too. For years, I've been exploring the idea of surrender, trying to get my head around it. For much of my life, I thought surrender meant giving up or giving in; being lazy, being out of control; living without purpose or direction; lacking motivation.

Over many years through many lessons, I've begun to understand the subtle power of surrender, the wisdom of it. The way that surrender is a posture of flexibility. That it's an essential aspect of the pulse of expansion and contraction that is built into our cells.

Surrender isn't about being out of control; it's not about being limp or aimless. The spirit of surrender is not forfeiture. It's not asking you to live without aims, goals or desires. It's not passive. It's not an invitation into victimhood or helplessness.

It's not weakness. It's wisdom.

Surrender is the ability to release resistance and respond skilfully. It's shedding your preferences in terrain where your preferences are irrelevant. It's relaxing your grip. It's the art of being with what is. Surrender is asking you to be in relationship with life. To move, palm to palm, hip to hip, with that aspect of life that is bigger than you.

When we resist or control or delude ourselves into thinking we can always take the lead, we miss the elegance, the alchemy. We don't see that the unexpected delights that deliver magic and joy, *and* the uninvited heartbreaks and hardships that baptise us, open our eyes to just how much capacity and strength we truly have.

When we embrace our powers of both purposefulness and surrender, we are more fully in conversation with life. And the more we refine our ability to shift gears gracefully between action and surrender (to lead and to follow, to speak and to listen, to move and to be still, to digest and to release, to work and to rest), the more our lives become a full expression of what is possible. The less we feel like life is happening to us and the more we recognise that our lives are a co-creation.

Surrender is what connects us to our source, empowers us and helps us live to our full potential. Surrender is what lets us dance with the divine. And sometimes that means letting life take the lead.

ELEVATE
your words to

ELEVATE
your life

E ver listen to yourself talk? If so, you've probably noticed the negative bias in the language you choose. By using phrases like 'I have to ...' or 'I need to ...' we add a weight and heaviness to our lives without even realising we're doing it. Not to mention the sneaky punk 'I am ...', which pigeonholes us into a particular (usually negative) emotional experience. The good news? It's just a habit and it can be easily changed.

What follows is a list of simple swaps you can make to instantly upgrade your experience of life. Not only will these swaps make you feel better right away, but when you make them a habit, you'll create a cumulative effect that equates to more gratitude, spaciousness and buoyancy in every day.

HAVE TO/GET TO

You could say, 'I have to exercise this morning.' Or upgrade that to 'I get to exercise this morning.' This swap shifts you into gratitude and reorients you to the absolute privilege it is to be able to move your body. It makes the whole idea inviting and light, rather than a heavy, obligatory burden. What a gift!

NEED TO/WANT TO

You could say, 'I need to write this article today.' Or upgrade that to 'I want to write this article today.' This swap shifts you into motivation and creates positive momentum by realigning you with the power of your desire. Letting your desires lead you is a lot easier than dragging obligation along behind you like a dead weight.

I AM/I FEEL

You could say, 'I am sad.' Or upgrade that to 'I feel sad.' This swap differentiates *you* from *the way you are feeling*, which reminds you that you are not your feelings. You *experience* your feelings and you are free to choose a different feeling anytime.

Today, if you notice yourself defaulting to 'have to' or 'need to', or boxing yourself in with 'I am', simply make the swap. It's a small but powerful tool to add to your kit. Elevate your words and you'll elevate your life, my friend!

LOOK FOR WHAT'S RIGHT, RIGHT NOW

LOOK FOR WHAT'S RIGHT, RIGHT NOW.

The human brain is designed to look for what's wrong. It's a survival strategy that served our species quite well in the past. But what about now? Is habitually looking for what's wrong serving you well?

In our modern lives, fear, criticism, anxiety and judgement are the lingering lenses of survival that create an illusion of safety. Negative perspectives are essentially damage control.

But how does it feel to live your life that way? Does it generate ideas? Open you up to opportunities? Create connections? Grow a sense of compassion? Awaken wonder within you? Keep you present and hopeful?

Or does it shut all that shit down?

The good news is, you are not your mind. You are not your thoughts. And you *are* 100 per cent able to retrain your attention and refine your mind. All that's necessary is to broaden your perspective to include the positive. It's an exercise in consciously including the things you habitually look through – the invisible good that, once you open your eyes to see it, is around you all the time. Goodness is flooding into your life at every moment; your critical mind has just made you blind to it.

So, how to retrain the mind and reclaim the goodness, the joy, the delight in your life? Start paying attention to what's right, right now.

Anytime you catch yourself noticing what's wrong, criticising, judging (yourself or others), worrying or projecting into the future, see if you can identify three things you're grateful for in that moment. Keep it small, specific and recent.

It sounds simple, but it's powerful enough to literally change your brain. A regular gratitude practice can be an effective way to develop a positive mindset – what Harvard happiness expert Shawn Achor calls 'the happiness advantage'.

Gratitude retrains your attention and broadens your perspective to include the positive. It helps you notice the things you might otherwise see through: the invisible goodness; those positive aspects of life that are so easily overlooked by a critical perspective.

So go and get grateful. Look around and ask yourself, 'What's right, right now?'

Maybe the obstacle is just pointing you towards higher ground

MAYBE THE OBSTACLE IS JUST POINTING YOU TOWARDS HIGHER GROUND.

M aybe the thing you think is a problem is actually an opportunity. Maybe the roadblock is rerouting you to a smoother path or one that can take you further. Maybe the obstacle is pointing you towards higher ground.

There are two kinds of people in this world: those who see problems and those who create solutions. The solution-makers are the true visionaries. They are the most resilient among us. They are the creative thinkers, the innovators, the natural leaders.

Maybe some of us are just born with that sense for problem-solving built in. But I believe that being solutions-focused and thinking positively is something we can cultivate in ourselves (and encourage in younger generations as well).

Because, really, a problem is just an opportunity. And if we start seeing our lives as being full of opportunities – rather than full of problems – we get to engage with our circumstances as change-makers, creatives and courageous pioneers, rather than powerless victims.

There are enough people in the world complaining about what isn't right. We need more people who see life through a lens of possibility – who see obstacles, problems and imperfections as puzzles to solve, as opportunities for innovation and evolution.

Naming the problem is easy. Solving the problem takes guts, empathy, creativity and courage.

Next time an obstacle crops up on your path, consider if it might be pointing you towards higher ground. See if you can engage with it through the lens of *possibility*.

KEEP YOUR INNER PEACE.

Your capacity for self-forgiveness, self-compassion, self-awareness and self-understanding directly influences your capacity to bring these qualities to your relationships with others. How you relate to *yourself* is how you relate to the *world*, and vice versa.

Next time you find yourself in a challenging or triggering situation, notice how you meet it. Notice what emotions you bring as you head into battle. Explore whether they are serving you or if they are just serving as a mirror reflecting how you feel about yourself. If you are waging a war within, you will always be at war with others. If you are at peace within yourself, you will always be at peace with others.

The energetic ripple effect of our inner lives radiates into our outer lives; there is no boundary or barrier. One more person who isn't suffering means one more person who isn't projecting that pain, anger or frustration onto others. One more person keeping the inner peace causes an exponential outward increase in loving kindness, compassion and understanding. This affects the manifestations of your outer life and your relationships with the people closest to you, obviously, but don't underestimate your impact. Your energetic imprint causes a ripple – it resonates and expands into your community and onwards, into the wider world. It counts. It matters.

Make peace your practice, starting with yourself. Be an inner activist first. Notice the internal dialogue, notice the (probably ample) opportunities to be kinder and more compassionate, tender and forgiving with yourself. Be softer with yourself. Give yourself a break, cut yourself some slack. Be curious. Smile, soften, relax back, expand. Make this your mission statement: peace begins with me. Keep your inner peace and you'll help create a peaceful world.

LOVE
BIG.
pass it on.

LOVE BIG. PASS IT ON.

W aking up to news stories of total devastation, an unexpected phone call delivering heartbreak or an email carrying a message of loss or illness can leave us feeling powerless, paralysed and fearful.

Here's the thing you can do right now: love more. Stop waiting for the world to change and start participating in creating change by loving more deeply and more freely.

Because acting from love will place you in a state of grace instead of a state of fear. Because love gives you a foothold when you feel like you're slipping, lost or afraid. Because showing love is a form of gratitude – and gratitude is the highest form of prayer. Because being loving reminds you of what really matters and what isn't important. Because acts of love reconnect you with your truest self. Because being loving is being compassionate – and compassion lifts the veil of our separateness. Because small acts of love add up to *big love*.

And because, ultimately, love is the answer.

Today, expand your heart to hold more. Say hello. Hug someone. Listen. Hold hands. Hold space. Kiss. Smile. Look people in the eye – all people. See yourself in them. Pay attention. Pay a compliment. Send a text. Pick up the phone. Pick up a piece of litter. Pick up the bill. Say 'thank you'. Say 'please'. Say 'yes'. Say 'I love you'. Say 'tell me more'. Say 'I want to understand'. Show your gratitude. Show compassion. Forgive. These are all small acts of love – tiny rebellions against suffering, injustice, separateness, pain, anxiety and fear.

The revolution of love starts with you. So uncage your heart. Put it on your sleeve. Liberate your love – give it freely and indiscriminately. You need it. We need it. The world needs it, now more than ever. Small acts of love every day keep the fear, shame and self-doubt away. *Love big.* Pass it on.

BLISS

IS A

BEACON

✳

BLISS IS A BEACON.

There are always times when we feel a little lost – about what we're here to do, about how to spend our days, about what our purpose is.

Here's the best advice I can give you: forget about what it looks like. Forget about all the 'shoulds' and 'coulds'. Forget about the degrees you have or don't have. Forget what makes sense.

Instead, pay attention to what feels good – to what makes your cells sing; to what lifts you up; to what fills up your cup; to what lights your fire, and leaves you feeling jazzed and alive and pumped up. These are all signs, signals and directions pointing the way to your true (fulfilled, satisfied, joyful, grateful) nature.

One of the best places to start is with your history. Go back to a time when you were allowed to play, to explore. Our childhood loves, interests and proclivities often leave us a breadcrumb trail back to our truest selves. Your history of bliss is a blueprint, a map home.

The easiest way to find the trail is to do something that brings a very familiar but perhaps long-forgotten bliss. Maybe walking in the woods or singing to the fields, collaging and creating, collecting stamps and bird nests, dressing up, dancing, writing stories, making music, riding bikes or horses, or, heck, even making mud pies.

Just think back to what you loved as a child and make a little list – an inventory of clues. Take your pick and hit the trail. Find your way back to your truest self by following the pointers left by your younger self. Your simplest, most innocent bliss is a beacon, pointing you back to your true nature, guiding your way home to wholeness.

When you do find those breadcrumbs of bliss left by your sweet baby self, take another clue from your childhood: be playful. Let it be an adventure. See where it takes you.

BE ALL OF YOU

BE ALL OF YOU.

You don't need to line up your personality perfectly or fit your beliefs into a box. Your dichotomous preferences, quirky combinations and mismatched inclinations do not mean you're confused, misguided or inconsistent. They are the many facets of one singular gem – the one-off personality mashup mixtape that only you can be. This crazy combo platter is where the youest you is – the *whole* you. And we (the world) love that shit, 'cause it's real and endearing and uniquely you. It's a whole lot more interesting than being predictable.

So come stand before the world, just as you are, without apology – in the full glory of your unique you-ness. Be funny and serious. Believe in spirit and in science. Be a part-time academic and a full-time dreamer. Be an artist and an accountant. Be beautiful and smart. Be innocent and wise. Be a mother and a wild woman. Be fierce and sweet. Love what you love, do what you do. Be boundless. Be borderless. Be weird. Be messy, magical, marvellous you.

Get out there and let all those funky facets of you shine and shimmer. Be all of you, so we can love all of you.

YOU ARE
WHAT YOU
WORSHIP

YOU ARE WHAT YOU WORSHIP.

Whatever you worship you become. So pay attention. Take note. Where do you direct your devotion on the daily? What are your rituals of reverence? What do you offer yourself to? What do you glorify?

Are you devoted to daily practices that uplift your life? Or are you in servitude to habits that tear you down? Is your daily ritual to plunge yourself into the whirlpool of social media, email and news – information overload, and an inevitable dynamic of comparison? Do you spend your days double-tapping pictures of airbrushed faces or bodies built on protein powder and diuretics? Do you worship at the altar of the digitised self? Do you spend your hours to-doing the shit out of your life, revering productivity and perfectionism, and offering yourself up to overwhelm?

Or do you devote yourself to presence and gratitude? Do you pay reverence to the richness of your inner life? Do you set your gaze upon things of true beauty? Do you fill your time with meaningful pursuits, nourishing endeavours and rituals that evoke joy? Is there space in your life for silence and stillness, gratitude and curiosity, wonder and laughter?

Open your eyes and notice. Pay attention to what fills you up, what lifts you up – and then notice whether you're creating a place of worship for that in your life.

Become mindful of how your devotion influences your life. Even the smallest rituals have big flow-on effects, for better or worse. You get to decide, because you become what you hold space for. You are what you worship.

GO WITHIN TO GET WHAT YOU NEED

GO WITHIN TO GET WHAT YOU NEED.

If you're feeling depleted, down in the dumps, uninspired, unsupported, unloved, unsure, not enough or just a little less-than ... go to the source. Go within to get what you need.

Nothing and no one outside of you can make you happier, more inspired, more loved, more beautiful or more complete than you are right now. No diet or relationship or credential or job or 'ideal' weight or piece of clothing will complete you. That's all on you.

All the feelings you're waiting for are already within you. All of the love, bliss and confidence you're wandering through life looking for are already within you, waiting to be unearthed, shaken loose and brought to light.

All of the answers you're looking for in life are already within you. Every single one. You are your own guru. The answers are buried within you like diamonds in a coal mine. They may be shrouded by self-doubt and second-guessing, but they are there, waiting for you to open your eyes and see them. It's all there – you just need to mine your inner resources.

The most effective way to go within and get what you need? Meditation. In meditation, we dive deep and awaken to the awe, intelligence, wisdom, divinity, beauty and majesty that already reside within us. We detach from the material, thinking world, from the barrage of information, and we tune in to our instincts and intuition. Meditation gifts us with inner alignment and inner resourcing; the ability to be clear about what is true, real and integral – what is aligned with our higher self. It gifts us the ability to source everything we need from within, to fill up our own cup and to alchemise darkness within us into light. It may sound like a miracle. It is. Try it for yourself. Commit to a daily meditation for seven days and watch what happens.

Go within to get what you need.

GET

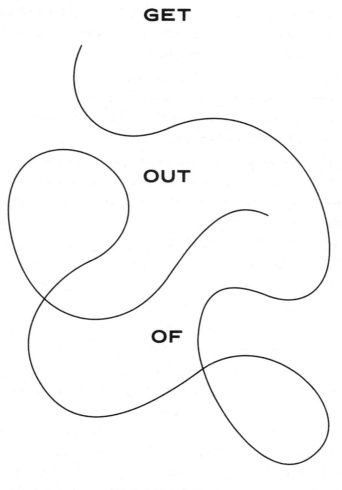

OUT

OF

CONTROL

G rasping, worrying, anxiety, fear and over-analysing are all ways we try to 'be in control'. We fool ourselves that worry is a failsafe insurance policy; that fear protects us in perpetuity; and that if we loosen our grip on the controls, we'll never become, achieve or receive.

In reality, when we are 'being in control' we aren't *being* at all. We aren't in conversation with our intuition. We aren't in a relationship with the universe or collective consciousness, or whatever it is that we define as the divine. We are cordoning ourselves off as finite, rather than recognising ourselves as part of the infinite.

In trying to control, we divert our attention away from presence. We fixate on the patterns of the past and fear of the future. We expend precious energy focusing on what we don't want, rather than what we do want. Ironically, we are diverting resources away from our desired outcomes. We are standing in the way, creating a blockade to the free flow of forward momentum in our lives.

When we try to control, we blind ourselves to possibility; we fall out of step with our best selves; we slip out of alignment with our highest good. We can't tell our intuition from our fear. We let our fear paralyse us, clinging to it long after it stopped serving us.

Being in a controlling state is exhausting and unsustainable. So this is a reminder: you have options. Get out of control. Swap 'being in control' for 'being in flow'. Step outside the circle of worry. Take a breath into your belly. Loosen your grip. Feel the freedom in that?

Remember that this life is a co-creation, that you are not alone. You are dancing with the divine. Your role is to be a good partner: flexible and intuitive, creative and courageous, both listening and leading in equal turns.

It's safe to trust yourself. It's safe to trust this life. Surrender yourself to the steps and watch how the divine dances with you, delivering you to your destiny.

Say it with me now: courageous, not controlling. Out of control, in flow.

TRUST

—

JUST

JUST

—

TRUST

JUST TRUST.

If you want to stress less (and be less fearful), trust more. Trust that you are safe. Trust yourself. Trust your gut. Trust your body. Trust that you're capable. Trust the timing. Trust the unfolding of things. Trust the messages. Trust that you will get what you need. Put your trust in people you love. Put your trust in the process. Infuse the intention of trust in all that you do.

When you make a practice of replacing feelings of fear ('I'm not safe, I'm not enough, I'm going to fail, all is not well, what if this happens, what if I can't ...') with trust, you soften, you relax, you put striving aside and move in graceful, sure-footed strides instead. You accomplish everything you want and need to, without the fretting, heartache, sleeplessness, anxiety, upset tummy, cortisol overload or jaw clenching.

To sidestep fear, start here: make *trust* your mantra today. Write it down, tattoo it on your heart, whisper it to yourself over and over again. When fear weasels its way into the conversation, block that bastard with a trust bomb. Blow up the fear with love. Make the choice. Make it a habit. Just trust.

LESS PUSH

more flow

LESS PUSH, MORE FLOW.

T hings don't always go to plan or according to schedule. We can't push the river – when it ain't flowin', it ain't flowin'. All that pushing leaves us exhausted, tapped out, dizzy with frustration and unfulfilled in that manic, spread-too-thin sense. So instead of being the river, be the riverbed. Let life flow through you.

Rivers are seasonal. So are we. There are juicy stages when expression, abundance and inspiration flow through us in great, dramatic gushes. There is the dazzling ecstasy of waterfalls; and there are dry-as-dust days, arid and parched, when nothing happens at all. There are times when we connect with the subtle elegance of a quiet but constant stream. There are moments of shadowy depth and afternoons of sun-speckled, ankle-deep wading. But it's all flow. It's all movement. It's all rhythm. And it's all good.

Embrace the seasons of your self. Be the vessel and let life flow through you. Less push, more flow.

REBEL

WITH A

PAUSE

I f stillness is hard for you, there's a reason for that. And you're not alone. Stillness opposes the way we are used to living – filling every moment with stimulation and information, earning our worth through busyness and accumulation. We've been trained to trade time for money, achievement for worthiness. We live in a culture that tells us we aren't enough – good enough, thin enough, smart enough, pretty enough, rich enough. That we must earn our worth. That our value is something to be bought, with either cash or the currency of achievement.

We've been conditioned into identifying who we are by what we have produced or purchased. We've mistaken products for personality and productivity for purpose. We've been set in a race against ourselves, running in hot pursuit of perfectionism and a finish line that doesn't exist.

The truth is that productivity and consumption are profitable for many and addictive for most (we're always chasing our next hit of worthiness). So there is no incentive, no permission, to stop, to slow down, to prioritise time over money and health over wealth. We feed the machine (and our habit) by staying on the hamster wheel: keep busy, keep hustling.

So it's unsurprising that we resist stillness; that quietude and spaciousness make us fidget; that we reject any endeavour with intangible outcomes, much less one that delivers us squarely into contentment and peace, no strings attached.

Stillness feels dangerous because it's the undoing of our misunderstanding that perfectionism and productivity are pathways to happiness. (Ironically, those are the very things that make us miserable.)

In this way, stillness (meditation in particular) is an act of rebellion. It is activism against a culture that has perpetuated speed, productivity, perfectionism and results at all costs. 'Just' being still and quiet with ourselves is rebelling against the things that make us miserable, sick, exhausted and broken. Stillness is a way of rewilding ourselves, of shaking free of the 'civilised' cultural constructs that keep us from our inner knowing, our innate wisdom and our inherent wholeness. All the doing in the world doesn't do that. Just being is the thing that frees us.

So if you want to stand up against the culture of busyness, productivity and perfectionism, sit the f*ck down. Rebel with a pause.

PRODUCTIVITY ISN'T THE ONLY WAY TO *measure* A DAY

PRODUCTIVITY ISN'T THE ONLY WAY TO MEASURE A DAY.

There are a million ways to measure a day. Productivity is only one of them. It's a valid one, but it's an overrated default.

Productivity is a handy metric. It makes our days feel quantifiable: itemised lists that we slay with tick marks; a full inbox that we wipe clean. Box ticking and inbox mastery make it easy to measure our efforts and make us feel like our days add up to something.

But here's the dark side of achievement: for many of us, achievement is a self-soothing mechanism. Productivity and achievement are cheap and convenient fillers, ways to top up our cup of self-worth. Box ticking temporarily pads out the hollows of our self-worth, laying a thin coat of worthiness on top of an abyss of emptiness (that vast, pervasive fear of 'I'm not enough').

While I'm all for being focused and making the most of our days, I think we could all use a reminder that productivity isn't the only way to measure a day – or, more to the heart of the matter, to measure self-worth.

So I present, for your consideration, a list of eleven less convenient (but far more meaningful) ways to measure our days:

* **Presence:** How present were you with the people you spent your day with? Did you listen well? Did you look them in the eye? Did you put down your phone when they were speaking to you? Did you find opportunities to single-task and make presence your primary focus?

* **Service:** Were you of service to others in some way? Did you show up for someone? Did you offer something? Did you give a gift or buy a coffee or lend a shoulder or rub a back? Did you volunteer your ear or make a meal or carry a bag of groceries? And how about *yourself*? Did you do something in service of your soul or your own self care?

* **Gratitude:** How much was there to be grateful for? What went well? What was beautiful? What was nourishing? >

* **Connection:** Did you have moments of true connection and intimacy with other humans? With yourself? Were you vulnerable and available?

* **Courage:** How much of your day was spent staying true to yourself? Did you prioritise your authenticity? Did you speak up? Did you put yourself out there? Did you stretch yourself and get outside of your comfort zone?

* **Truth:** How clearly did you speak your truth? Did you honour others' truths? Did you see the truth in a situation, regardless of whether it was in disagreement with your preferences or personal comfort?

* **Empathy:** Did you find occasion to put yourself in someone else's shoes (especially before jumping to conclusions)? Did you consider others' perspectives?

* **Forgiveness:** Did you forgive yourself well and often? Did you put petty bullshit to bed and forgive others fully?

* **Recognition:** Did you tell someone how much you care about them, how they made a difference in your day, how much they matter? Did you feel loved? Did you feel seen? Did you seize every opportunity to recognise others? Did others recognise *you* in ways big or small today?

* **Generosity:** Did you share what you have? Did you leave a fat tip? Did you go the extra mile? Did you give your gifts?

* **Joy:** F*ck yeah, joy! How many hidden treasures of happiness did you unearth today? How many milliseconds of bliss? How many moments of remembering your freedom, your agency and the big f*cking stroke of luck you had just by being born? Did you laugh (ideally at your own jokes)? Did you crack a smile? Tally up the joy.

Now *that's* the way to measure a life that matters.

trust

in

rest

TRUST IN REST.

Rest is wildly underrated. Emptiness is totally undervalued. Pauses are sacred spaces. *Stopping sometimes* is truly the secret sauce to a richer life. Because when we pause and sink in, we reconnect with the depths of ourselves – and it is from those depths that inspiration, creativity, wisdom, clarity and potency spring forth.

Although resting should be second nature to us, we've learned to override the signals. In doing so habitually, we've lost our trust in rest. Many of us actually fear rest and have to be forced into it. We miss the signs that it's time to lay down the doing, and we fumble into rest by way of illness and burnout.

Why do we fear rest? Because achievement is the addiction du jour in our culture. We avoid anxious feelings by keeping our pipelines full and tasks piled high. If we stay busy, we don't have to sit with discomfort. Every little achievement rewards us with a cheap hit of worthiness. Beneath all that bustling and busyness and box ticking, we are afraid we are not enough just as we are. So it's no wonder that stopping and resting can be hard. It's no wonder we don't transition into rest with much grace.

The good news is: instead of letting rest 'happen' to us out of necessity, we can learn to welcome it. Creating intentional pauses (both short and long) in our lives carves out opportunities for rest, reflection and renewal.

The more comfortable we are with cycling through periods of rest, the less we resist it. The less we resist rest, the more we benefit from it. Those benefits build our trust in rest – and in ourselves.

How can you invite periods of rest and stillness into your day, week, month, year? How can you stop resisting this part of the energetic cycle and, instead, start honouring it?

SELF-CARE
IS SACRED

SELF-CARE IS SACRED.

I think the phrases 'self-love' and 'self-care' sound a bit ... limp. Less than inspiring. Boring even. Like, 'Oh great, another thing I need to do.' *Am I right?*

Here's my hack: add the word 'sacred' as a prefix and, suddenly, I'm more interested. Sacred self-care sounds like something I can get down with. It doesn't feel mundane or laborious. It sounds *divine*.

And it *is*.

If you subscribe to the fact that you are part of divinity (whether it's that you're made of stardust, your body is a vessel for the soul or a higher being had a hand in your creation), who are you *not* to take care of your divine self? Who are you to wear down your divinity with no maintenance, no conscious care and no love?

When you reframe self-care as a sacred act, you give yourself permission: permission to recognise how important it actually is; permission to prioritise your own wellbeing as a divine being; permission to ditch the guilt and actually enjoy – and even be proud of – taking care of yourself.

Take note: if you battle with feeling selfish and guilty when faced with an opportunity for self-care, you are not alone. Our culture has trained us not to look after ourselves. So when that guilt pops up (and it will), short-circuit it with this reality check: when you fill up your cup, you have more to give. Sacred self-care gives you the resources to show up as your best self in your life (versus as a frazzled, exhausted, impatient shadow of yourself). And when you're moving through life as a well-cared-for human being, that means you can, in turn, truly care well for others.

So go on with your divine self and get some *sacred* self-care happening in your life. You deserve it. We all do.

WORRY   IS

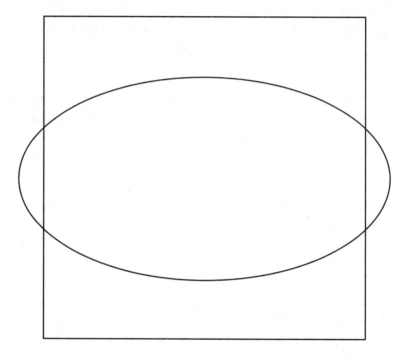

A   WASTE

WORRY IS A WASTE.

A gentle reminder: worry is a damn waste.

Worry zaps your time, your attention, your energy and your creativity. Worry yields nothing. It solves nothing. It creates nothing – other than wickedly spawning more and more worries to contend with.

Worry diverts your attention away from receptivity, creativity and solutions. It drains your reserves of energy as you cycle through the worst-case scenarios, stripping away your ability to perceive possibility.

Worry gnaws away at your stores of strength and corrodes your confidence with its repetitive droning, 'What if, what if, what if ...'

Of course worry has a point to make. Is this life mysterious? Yes. Is there so much that is unknown? Absolutely. Do we have precious little control over what comes next? Truly.

But rather than fearing the future, dreading the unknown or futilely grasping for control, what if you embrace the mystery of it all? What if you meet all the things you're worrying about with a little more curiosity, a little more hope, a little more wonder?

What if it all works out? What if it's going to be better than you imagined? What if you use your creative power to envisage something wonder-full rather than something worry-full?

At best, you'll align yourself with positive outcomes. At the very least, you'll preserve your energy, refine your ability to direct your attention and keep an eye out for wonderful new possibilities.

Worry is a waste. So forget it.

Forget worrying. Start wondering.

PEACE
PEACE
PEACE
PEACE
OUT
OUT
OUT
OUT

PEACE OUT.

Offering a little loving kindness to the world reconnects us with our humanity, reminds us of our kinship and helps us lean in to compassion and connection – rather than judgement and separation. Blissful bonus: the more compassion you offer others, the more you will have to offer yourself. Less judgement and less perfectionistic punishment add up to more happiness and joy for all.

So today, why not take a beat to make an offering from the heart and drop a bliss bomb of benevolence into the world? It's simple to do. With your eyes closed, focus your attention on someone in the world who could do with a dose of love, tenderness and compassion. It could be someone you know who is going through a challenging time, a group of people who are suffering or just a general wish for the world. (It might even be someone who you have a beef with. That's black-belt shit, but it's magic. Try it and watch how it transforms your feels.)

Whoever is the benefactor of your blessing today, hold them in your heart for a moment and direct love their way. For you, this might take shape as a feeling, visualising light around them or simply repeating a blessing like, 'May they be happy, may they be well, may they feel safe, may they feel free.'

Send a *peace out*, in whatever way feels most natural to you.

these
are
the
good
old
days

THESE ARE THE GOOD OLD DAYS.

Take a breath. Are you rushing through the moment?

Are you postponing your happiness until some future point you're waiting for? Stop. Stop postponing your joy!

Step off that treadmill of tomorrows and arrive in this moment – this moment that, right now, is offering itself to you. It's yours. Seize it. Shape it. Make it into something beautiful. Make this moment memorable. Make it matter.

Because the truth is that these *are* the good old days, and memories are made in the present.

SELF-TRUST IS DIVINE

SELF-TRUST IS DIVINE.

I once heard the luminous Taryn Toomey say, 'Control is a man-made structure. Trust is a divine structure.'

I love this idea: this juxtaposition of control and trust, of human and divine. It's understanding that control is a human construct – a grasping, a striving, often based in self-preservation (at best) and fear (at worst). Control is something we humans reach for constantly, despite knowing that we can access so very little of it.

Trust, on the other hand, offers a way to be in *relationship* with the divine. It's a way to connect with something so much greater than ourselves; a way to co-create our lives. Trusting invites us to recognise divinity – and, thereby, our own humility. Controlling seeks to defy both of those ideas.

Here's the really beautiful thing about trust as it relates to the unfolding of our lives: our inner wisdom is connected to the greater wisdom of universal consciousness – the divine. In listening to our own best guidance, we're taking our cues from the divine. Paradoxically, by trusting ourselves we are tuning in to and trusting something much, much bigger than ourselves. To trust ourselves is to trust the divine.

There's a lot of humility in that – a lot of grace, a lot of reverence – and very little control.

My! How humbling to be in relationship with creation itself! How very small it makes us feel.

And yet, how powerful.

Take a breath before you say

'YES'

I believe being of service should be everyone's primary intention in life. We should all be thinking about how we can give, how we can lift others up and how we can contribute to our communities.

But it can be easy to teeter off the edge of being of service and land squarely in the territory of people pleasing, where the perpetual soundtrack is 'If I don't help people, they won't love me'; 'If they're not okay, I'm not okay'; 'If I don't show up for everything, I'm not worth anything.'

If that sounds familiar, you might be using your usefulness as a way to validate your ego. If you're addicted to positive feedback, to being needed or to taking responsibility for everyone else's feelings all the time, you might have mixed up being of service with servicing your self-esteem.

The danger here? You lose your ability to discern when being of service to others is actually letting yourself down. (If 'no' isn't in your vocabulary, I'm lookin' at you!) Being of service to others shouldn't cost you your health, your sanity or your ability to care for yourself. Perfectionism disguised as altruism is still perfectionism.

Here's the challenge: saying yes feels so good. That's why we do it so often (for most of us, too often). Saying yes has become our default because it's rewarding and affirming (in the short-term). It just sort of slips out of our mouths, and then we get an instant hit: a people-pleasing power-up, if you will. It's like a sugar high: a cheap thrill, hard to resist, usually followed by a hangover of regret. When the 'yes' is authentic and aligned with our highest good, it doesn't feel that way. But mostly, we say yes as an impulse – not a considered, intentional response.

And now, a tool to liberate yourself from a cycle of incessant 'yeses': next time you find yourself about to say yes, take a breath. Insert a momentary pause to consider this: are you saying yes because you genuinely want to do what is being asked of you? Because it feels good, you can, you want to and you need nothing in return – not even an acknowledgment or thank you? (Note: this is *love*.) Or are you saying yes because you want the person to like you, perceive you in a certain way or validate you? (Note: this is *fear*.) Check in with the resonance. Is it a 'yes' of love or fear? If it's born of fear, you probably need to flip that 'Y' to an 'N'. >

Other questions that might be helpful:

Does this feel like something I can do without encroaching on my own boundaries (of time, energy, resources or integrity)? Or am I violating my boundaries to offer this 'yes'?

How will I feel *after* I say yes? Will I have a 'yes' hangover and kick myself later for committing to something I don't really want to do, or don't really have the time, energy or resources for?

Do I need to be acknowledged for what I'm saying yes to, or is the act self-fulfilling?

And, finally, a prayer for all the 'yes' junkies in the crowd: may you breathe deeply into your belly before saying yes and, in doing so, be reminded of the difference between being of service and being a people pleaser.

YOU ARE A GALAXY OF POSSIBILITY

YOU ARE A GALAXY OF POSSIBILITY.

Your bones are built of stardust. You hold starlight in your cells. Just as you are contained by the universe, the universe is contained within you.

You are a galaxy of possibility. Alive, dancing within an even wider galaxy of possibility. You are self-luminous, endowed with the heat and surety of the stars.

Truth, wisdom and purpose are alive in you, alight in you. *You are cosmic potential.*

Remember the limitlessness of your lineage, your ancestry of stars. Knowing you are star-born, how can you expand your vocabulary of possibility today?

be

hope

a

dealer

Resources

HEAVILY MEDITATED APP

Download the Heavily Meditated app for free access to complementary companion practices to *The Hope Dealer*. You'll find guided meditations, journalling prompts and yoga nidra practices to support you to connect with a sense of positivity, possibility and trust so that you can tune in to your highest, most hopeful self and plug in to your full potential every day!

heavilymeditatedapp.com

THE HOPE DEALER DOWNLOADS

Here you'll find some fun, free downloads of messages from the book – yours to save, print and share. My gift to you.

caitlincady.com/the-hope-dealer-bonuses

Gratitude

To you, the reader. Thank you for the privilege of your attention. Your eyes on these words matter and your resonance creates deep meaning in my life. I am humbled. I am grateful.

To the incredible Dani Hunt at Neverland Studio. My creative compadre, the designer of my dreams, the mustard to my blush, the Oswald to my Lust Pro. Thank you for bringing yet another idea to life with me. Your creative flair and eye for detail are second to none. You elevate everything you touch and I'm so lucky to create with you.

To my publisher Kelly Doust, a writer in her own right, a woman with great vision and keen instincts, thank you for the opportunities you have offered me. I am truly grateful for your wise counsel, your advocacy and your grace. I feel so lucky to finally work with you. Long may it last!

To my editors Brooke Lyons, Kevin O'Brien and Laura Franks, and my proofreader Emma Schwarcz, thank you for your kindness, your care and your diligence.

To the everyone at Affirm Press and Hay House, thank you so much for gracing me with the space to share what I can. It is an honour and a privilege and a dream come true. A special thank you to Sally Mason-Swaab at Hay House and Linda Kaplan at Kaplan/DeFiore Rights for helping to bring this book to readers in the US and UK. I am forever grateful.

To the marvellous Maddy Cornelius, thank you for being an integrator extraordinaire and corralling my untamed punctuation. I appreciate you.

To my mother, Lisa and and my late father Tracey. You are both shining examples of hope and resilience. Thank you. I am who I am because of you.

To Loren, my steady, strong, fiercely loving and loyal husband. I couldn't do any of this without you by my side. I carry your heart.

And finally, to my wise little wildlings, Oliver, Isla and Hanalei, thank you for keeping me in touch with wonder, awe and play. I love you, sweet babies. xx

big

good

high

ove

vibes

opes

CONNECT WITH

HAY HOUSE
ONLINE

🌐 hayhouse.co.uk   **f** @hayhouse

📷 @hayhouseuk   🐦 @hayhouseuk

▶ @hayhouseuk   ♪ @hayhouseuk

Find out all about our latest books & card decks • Be the first to know about exclusive discounts • Interact with our authors in live broadcasts • Celebrate the cycle of the seasons with us • Watch free videos from your favourite authors • Connect with like-minded souls

'*The gateways to wisdom and knowledge are always open.*'

Louise Hay